Fresh Expressions in the Mission of the Church

Report of an Anglican-Methodist
Working Party

Church House Publishing
Church House
Great Smith Street
London SW1P 3AZ

ISBN 978 0 7151 4295 0
GS 1871
DL626-CT-12

Published 2012 for the General Synod of the Church of England by Church
House Publishing

Printed in England by
CPI Group (UK) Ltd, Croydon, CRO 4YY

Contents

Abbreviations

ARCIC	Anglican-Roman Catholic International Commission
BEM	*Baptism, Eucharist and Ministry*
CLP	*Called to Love and Praise*
NCC	*The Nature and Mission of the Church*
MWB	*Methodist Worship Book*
WCC	World Council of Churches

Membership of the Working Party

For the Church of England:
The Right Revd Alan Smith (Co-Chair)
The Revd Canon Professor Loveday Alexander
Dr Martin Davie
Dr Rachel Jordan
The Revd Canon Dr Roland Riem

For the Methodist Church
Mr David Walton (Co-Chair)
The Revd Dr David M. Chapman
Ms Christine Elliott
The Revd Graham Horsley
The Revd Dr Peter Phillips
The Revd Dr Angela Shier-Jones*

Consultants:
The Right Revd Graham Cray
The Revd Stephen Lindridge

*The Revd Dr Angela Shier-Jones was appointed to the working party and attended its initial meetings. Sadly, Angela died in August 2011 following a serious illness. Members of the working party wish to acknowledge with gratitude her colleagueship and scholarship.

Foreword

One of the big encouragements of the first years of the twenty-first century has been the impetus of Christians to discover new ways of living out and communicating the Gospel in a restless and sceptical age. This has brought with it a number of challenges and questions, not least about what it means to be the Church – and how these 'fresh expressions' relate to what have been termed 'inherited' forms of the Church. This report does not attempt a comprehensive review of the ecclesiology of either approach: it does however seek to crystallize some of the major questions and to provide a number of pointers as to how together we may grapple creatively with them.

One of the most valuable aspects of the process has been the opportunity for Anglicans and Methodists to work together on this common task. We are grateful for the significant variety of experience and insight which members of the Group have brought to our work; in particular those who have undertaken the tasks of writing and editing. We wish to pay special tribute to the contribution of Angela Shier-Jones, who died during the final stage of the Report's preparation; she brought an incisive mind and her own stimulating theological insights to our deliberations and she is sadly missed.

This report has concentrated on those areas of fresh expressions which Anglicans and Methodists have in common. We are aware that this approach has meant that there are some areas which each church will need to go on exploring further.

For Methodists there is more to be said about *Venture FX* than we have included in this report. This creative programme has seen the appointment of a cohort of pioneer ministers – both lay and ordained – who are working in a wide variety of geographical and cultural settings. There are also some more general questions for Methodism as it looks afresh at what it means to be a *Connexional* church in the contemporary context.

Anglicans will wish to reflect further on the role of bishops as the focus of unity and the leader in mission in a diocese as they encourage fresh expressions to develop. *Bishops' Mission Orders* are just one of the new avenues that have opened up creative ways of allowing a more strategic approach to fresh expressions. Over the past few years there have been many exciting new initiatives in Church of England schools, which are helping us think creatively about ecclesiology. Among Anglicans there is also much interest in *new monasticism* which is raising some fascinating questions about the nature of the Church.

We are convinced that there is an important task of listening and a sharing of experience which needs to flow from this Report; also a sense that 'inherited' and 'fresh' expressions of the Church will be more effective as they learn from each other what it is to be a sign of God's kingdom in the world. We hope that this will further the mission and ministry of our two churches and also help us work together more closely under the Covenant.

1

Fresh Expressions and the Church

1.1 Fresh Expressions

1.1.1   The Church of England and the Methodist Church of Great Britain share in a common mission to proclaim the Gospel of Jesus Christ in ways that take account of the circumstances and needs of contemporary British society. While social and theological commentators differ among themselves in their analysis of the current situation, there is a substantial body of opinion among Christians that the steep decline in participation in mainstream Church life in Britain throughout the second half of the twentieth century, combined with the increasing secularisation of Western society, calls for an innovative approach to Christian mission in the twenty-first century.

1.1.2   The publication in 2004 of the Church of England report *Mission-Shaped Church: church planting and fresh expressions of church in a changing context* was a landmark in the development of a new strategy for Christian mission in Britain by Anglicans, Methodists and others.[1] A direct outcome of the report was the setting up of the ecumenical Fresh Expressions initiative, which has since led to the development of 'fresh expressions of church' (or simply 'fresh expressions') in a large number of Anglican parishes and Methodist circuits.

---

1 *Mission-Shaped Church: church planting and fresh expressions of church in a changing context* (London: Church House Publishing, 2004).

1.1.3   As defined by the Fresh Expressions initiative:
A fresh expression is a form of church for our changing culture, established primarily for the benefit of people who are not yet members of any church:

- It will come into being through principles of listening, service, incarnational mission and making disciples;
- It will have the potential to become a mature expression of church shaped by the gospel and the enduring marks of the church and for its cultural context.[2]

1.1.4   The Methodist Church was represented in the working party that produced *Mission-Shaped Church* and subsequently endorsed its recommendations by becoming an enthusiastic partner with the Church of England in the Fresh Expressions initiative. 'Encouraging fresh ways of being Church' is ranked among the *'Priorities for the Methodist Church'*.[3]

1.1.5   Throughout this present report, 'Fresh Expressions' written with capital letter refers to the official ecumenical initiative; whereas 'fresh expressions' written in lower case refers to individual mission projects within either the Church of England or the Methodist Church which come under the umbrella of the Fresh Expressions initiative.

1.1.6   While some theological commentators regard fresh expressions as part of a wider phenomenon generally known as 'emerging church', there are important distinctions to be made between the two. Since there are no commonly agreed definitions, this present report reserves the term 'fresh expression' to refer to those mission projects sponsored by one of the denominations participating in the Fresh Expressions initiative, as distinct from post-denominational

---

2 From the website 'Share: Exploring fresh expressions of church together': http://www.sharetheguide.org/section1/1.
3 *Encouraging fresh ways of being Church* (Methodist Conference report, 2004).

mission projects led by independent groups and individuals, some of whom are disaffected with the historic churches. It is these latter communities that are referred to here as 'emerging church'. Such communities are more common in North America, where post-denominationalism is an established feature of the religious land-scape, though the phenomenon is becoming increasingly common in Britain. Since fresh expressions are intended to be new forms of church within one of the historic churches in Britain, it is potentially misleading to regard them as part of the emerging church scene.

1.2 Practical questions arising from fresh expressions

1.2.1   The existence of fresh expressions in the Church of England and the Methodist Church gives rise to a number of practical questions, as the following general examples illustrate:

- An Anglican fresh expression for bikers operates across the whole of an Anglican Deanery. How does its ministry relate to the ministry of the parish churches in the deanery, each of which seeks to offer a pastoral ministry to the people living in its parish?
- A Methodist fresh expression ministering to the surfing community in a coastal resort would like to start celebrating Holy Communion on a regular basis. Should it be obliged to observe Methodist discipline concerning presidency at Holy Communion or should its lay leaders be permitted to preside because of their relationship with the community?
- A confirmation service at an Anglican fresh expression involves a celebration of the Eucharist at which all are invited to receive the bread and wine. As a result, several people who have not been baptised receive the bread and wine. While this 'open table' approach is contrary to Church of England practice, is it perhaps a justifiable exception on a particular occasion where it might have evangelistic benefit?

• A fresh expression in a Methodist circuit results in a flourishing ministry to young people. Should that fresh expression be regarded as a youth work project of the circuit or as a church in its own right?

1.3 Theological questions arising from fresh expressions

1.3.1 Behind these practical questions lie important theological questions concerning the nature of the Christian Church, its structures and authorized forms of ministry. Some of these questions were already foreseen in *Mission-Shaped Church*; others have been posed subsequently. The following list is not intended to be exhaustive but illustrates the kind of theological questions about the Church which arise in relation to fresh expressions of church.

• Can fresh expressions properly be regarded as churches or are they Christian communities that have the potential to become churches?
• If fresh expressions are churches as such, are they entirely new forms of the Church for the twenty-first century or are they re-formed, renewed or purified manifestations of existing forms of the Church?
• If fresh expression are not churches as such but have the potential to become churches, by what process and at what point in their development do they become churches in the true sense of the term?
• Can a Christian community properly be described as being a fresh expression of church without it necessarily also being *a* church?
• How do fresh expressions relate to Anglican parish churches or local Methodist churches in the overall mission and ministry of the Church of England and the Methodist Church?
• Given that the Church of England and the Methodist Church have been shaped by their respective histories, how might

4

fresh expressions develop a spiritual and sacramental life in a way that respects what has been received from the past, while recognising and affirming their pioneering context?

- To what extent is it appropriate to interpret fresh expressions as part of an historical pattern of renewal movements that arise from time to time in the life of the Church in response to changing circumstances?

- Alternatively, to what extent is it appropriate to interpret fresh expressions as an unprecedented and radical innovation in the life of the Church such that they require the development of an entirely new theological understanding of the Church?

- What theological (and practical) implications do fresh expressions hold for the way in which the Church of England and the Methodist Church currently justify the deployment of scarce resources of authorized ministers and finance?

- What theological (and practical) issues of accountability arise in relation to fresh expressions?

1.4 The task of the working party

1.4.1   This present report is presented to the General Synod of the Church of England and to the Methodist Conference by the Joint Anglican-Methodist Working Party on the Ecclesiology of Emerging Expressions of Church. In the spirit of joint collaboration envisaged in the Anglican-Methodist Covenant, this working party was convened under the auspices of the Church of England's Faith and Order Advisory Group (now the Faith and Order Commission) and the Methodist Faith and Order Committee to investigate the explicit and implicit theological understanding of the Church which underpins fresh expressions.[4] It cannot be stated too strongly that an evaluation of the Fresh Expressions initiative is beyond the remit of the working party.

---

4 The precise origins of the working party and its terms of reference are set out in Appendix 1.

1.4.2   The members of the working party wish to record their gratitude for the assistance received from those members of the Fresh
Expressions leadership team who have been consulted in preparing
this report. We have been impressed by the way in which they and
fresh expressions practitioners are willing to engage with the theological issues arising from their work. It is evident that the Fresh
Expressions initiative is inspired by a deep concern for the vitality
of the Church of England and the Methodist Church, and by a
strong desire to engage in Christian mission among that substantial
section of the population for whom Anglican parish churches and
local Methodist churches are unattractive.

1.4.3   As has already been noted, since 'fresh expressions' is still a
relatively new term, there is as yet no commonly accepted vocabulary in place. Therefore, as a contribution towards the development of a standard vocabulary, as well as to assist the reader, the
working party has compiled a glossary of key terms as they feature
in this report.[5]

1.4.4   It is fair to say that, in a short period of time, *Mission-
Shaped Church* and Fresh Expressions have generated a significant
amount of secondary literature from supporters and critics alike.[6]
Judging by the passionately held convictions expressed in much of
this material, Anglicans and Methodists are far from indifferent
towards Christian mission in contemporary British society, though
opinion remains divided concerning what constitutes an appropriate mission strategy.

1.4.5   Regrettably, the entirely legitimate debate about fresh expressions easily becomes muddied by mutual suspicion, vested interest and divergent perspectives. For instance, fresh expressions
practitioners sometimes express concern that their communities
are subject to far greater scrutiny than Anglican parish churches

---

5 See Appendix 2.
6 See the select bibliography at the end of this report.

or local Methodist churches. Conversely, critics of *Mission-shaped Church* sometimes express concern that the prevailing climate within the Church of England and the Methodist Church discourages objective scrutiny of fresh expressions. Such concerns on either side may not be wholly without foundation. Nevertheless, all parties to the debate must be willing to acknowledge the integrity of positions other than their own.

1.4.6 Following a reference by the Archbishop of Canterbury, Rowan Williams, it has become commonplace for Anglicans (and Methodists) to talk of a 'mixed economy' whereby fresh expressions and Anglican parish churches (or local Methodist churches) co-exist and co-operate in advancing the Church's mission.[7] Opinion among commentators is divided as to whether and how fresh expressions can properly be regarded as churches in the true sense of the term. Some commentators (and many practitioners) readily describe fresh expressions as new or alternative forms of the Church on an equal basis with Anglican parish churches or local Methodist churches. Other commentators, while affirming in principle the value of fresh expressions within a broad mission strategy, believe that they lack some or very many of the essential ecclesial elements that make them recognizable as churches in the true sense of the term.

1.4.7 The difference between these positions is theologically more significant than a mere matter of terminology. It concerns the ecclesial reality of fresh expressions within the Church of England or the Methodist Church. If a fresh expression can properly be said to be '*a* church', then it must contain the fullness of the universal Church and thus contain everything that is required to sustain a spiritual and sacramental life in communion with other local churches. If a fresh expression cannot properly be said to be a church, then it

---

7 The term 'mixed economy' was coined by Archbishop Rowan Williams when he was Archbishop of Wales. In a foreword to the Church in Wales report *Good News in Wales*, he wrote: 'We may discern signs of hope . . . These may be found particularly in the development of a mixed economy of Church life . . . there are ways of being church alongside the inherited parochial pattern.' Cited in *Mission-Shaped Church*, p. 26.

must lack the fullness of the universal Church and thus lack some of the essential elements that are required to sustain a complete spiritual and sacramental life in communion with other Christian communities.

1.4.8   The question of whether it is appropriate to describe a fresh expression as a church is very sensitive. To say that a fresh expression is not a church in the true sense of the term would appear to involve an adverse judgement. For this reason, fresh expressions practitioners are often reluctant to accept that fresh expressions may not be churches. However, without prejudging the matter, such a conclusion need not be interpreted negatively. On the contrary, it would enable the Church of England and the Methodist Church to determine how fresh expressions can acquire the ecclesial elements that together would identify them as churches.

1.4.9   This joint Anglican-Methodist Working Party is acutely aware of the strongly expressed convictions relating to fresh expressions. The members of the working party themselves represent different theological perspectives, though each brings relevant expertise and experience to its appointed work. Collectively and individually, members of the working party recognize that it is their duty to investigate the ecclesiological or 'churchly' nature of fresh expressions in a way that is impartial, thorough and constructive.

1.4.10   The particular task before the working party in this present report is to state the criteria by which it is possible for the Church of England and the Methodist Church to recognize fresh expressions as churches, according to their respective teaching concerning the nature of the Church. It is for those who exercise a ministry of oversight to determine the extent to which a particular fresh expression actually fulfils those criteria. Again, this kind of judgement need not be interpreted in a negative sense. A fresh expression that does not possess all the essential elements of the Church may still develop in a way that leads towards this objective or else legitimately continue as a mission project.

1.4.11   Although the working party necessarily focuses its attention on fresh expressions, this does not mean that such communities are more in need of scrutiny than Anglican parish churches or local Methodist churches. The working party neither makes nor implies any value judgement on fresh expressions. For the purpose of this present report, it is not the quality or effectiveness of Christian mission represented by an individual fresh expression that is at issue, but whether and how a fresh expression has, or might acquire, those elements that enable it properly to be called a church, as this term is understood and used by the Church of England and the Methodist Church.

1.4.12   The working party does not intend to address ecclesiological issues raised by the widespread use of the internet for spiritual and religious purposes. The intriguing idea of 'virtual' or 'internet' church therefore lies beyond the scope of this present report. The Methodist Church has established a separate working party to address this issue.

1.5 Reference point for theological reflection on the Church

1.5.1   The reference point or corner stone for theological reflection on the nature of fresh expressions in relation to the Church is provided by the respective doctrinal standards of the Church of England and the Methodist Church. While this may seem obvious, it needs to be stated because of a possible tendency to assume that the nature of the Church is an entirely open question among Anglicans and Methodists. On the contrary, the Church of England and the Methodist Church each has its official standard of teaching concerning the Church itself.

1.5.2   Nevertheless, some would argue that doctrinal standards formulated in previous generations should not be permitted to constrain current developments that are manifestly inspired by the Holy Spirit. The situation in which these doctrinal standards were originally formulated, it is suggested, was very different to that facing the Church today. The contemporary context of Christian mission in Britain calls for a radical departure from the past in favour of an innovative theological understanding of the Church and its mission, in keeping with the needs of the present age.

1.5.3   From this perspective, the doctrinal legacy inherited from previous generations should be set aside so that new forms of the Church can develop under the inspiration of the Holy Spirit. Those who adopt this position often distinguish between so-called 'inherited' or 'traditional' church and 'emerging' church, of which fresh expressions are thought to be one particular strand.

1.5.4   Such an argument, on examination, is seen to be flawed. The Church does not receive its identity exclusively, or even primarily, from contemporary theological reflection in response to the perceived realities of a particular missionary context. Essentially, the Church is a divine creation, whose nature is a matter of belief. Anglicans and Methodists profess their faith using the words of the Nicene Creed: 'We believe in one, holy, catholic and apostolic Church.' The respective doctrinal standards of the Church of England and the Methodist Church are intended to preserve their belief concerning this one, holy, catholic and apostolic Church. Thus the doctrinal standards state the criteria by which Anglicans and Methodists respectively can be confident that a particular Christian community is *visibly* and *recognizably* a church, in which is present the one, holy, catholic and apostolic Church. Adherence to the doctrinal standards is intended to guard against developments that would compromise the integrity of the Church.

1.5.5   For these reasons, the doctrinal standards of the Church of England and the Methodist Church are not to be discarded as irrelevant at the present juncture. Not all practical or theological trends among Christians can be attributed uncritically to the inspiration of the Holy Spirit. The Church of England and the Methodist Church have a duty to test the various spirits at work in the life of the Church (1 John 4.1–6) in order to discern the guidance of the Holy Spirit. One of the purposes of this present report is to contribute to that process of discernment, which properly belongs to the authorized ministries of oversight in the Church of England and the Methodist Church.

1.5.6   It would be incorrect to suppose that the doctrinal standards of the Church of England and the Methodist Church impose a strait-jacket on discernment so that only traditional forms of the Church could ever be recognized as such. On the contrary, the doctrinal standards of both churches provide a degree of flexibility when it comes to identifying where the Church is concretely located in the world. Thus the working party must determine whether and how the doctrinal standards of the Church of England and the Methodist Church could permit fresh expressions to be identified as particular churches, and equally whether and how the existence of fresh expressions prompts new interpretations of these doctrinal standards.

1.5.7   Since the doctrinal standards of the Church of England and the Methodist Church are central to the study being undertaken in this present report, we now turn our attention to them before describing the theological method adopted in the report.

1.6 Doctrinal standards: the Church of England

1.6.1   The doctrinal standards of the Church of England are set out in Canons A5 and C15. Canon A5, 'Of the Doctrine of the Church of England', states that:

The doctrine of the Church of England is grounded in the Holy Scriptures, and in such teachings of the ancient Fathers and Councils of the Church as are agreeable to the said Scriptures. In particular such doctrine is to be found in the Thirty-Nine Articles of Religion, the Book of Common Prayer, and the Ordinal.

1.6.2   Canon C15, 'Of the Declaration of Assent', contains a declaration made by ordained ministers and some authorized lay ministers at the start of their ministry or when taking up a new appointment. This Canon begins with a short Preface that explains the self-understanding of the Church of England:

The Church of England is part of the One, Holy, Catholic and Apostolic Church worshipping the one true God, Father, Son and Holy Spirit. It professes the faith uniquely revealed in the Holy Scriptures and set forth in the catholic creeds, which faith the Church is called upon to proclaim afresh in each generation. Led by the Holy Spirit, it has borne witness to Christian truth in its historic formularies, the Thirty-nine Articles of Religion, the Book of Common Prayer and the Ordering of Bishops, Priests and Deacons. In this declaration you are about to make will you affirm your loyalty to this inheritance of faith as your inspiration and guidance under God in bringing the grace and truth of Christ to this generation and making Him known to those in your care?

In response to this Preface, the person making the Declaration of Assent then replies:

I, *A.B*, do so affirm, and accordingly declare my belief in the faith which is revealed in the Holy Scriptures and set forth in the catholic creeds and to which the historic formularies of the Church of England bear witness; and in public prayer and administration of the sacraments, I will use only the forms of service that are authorized or allowed by Canon.

1.6.3   Subordinate to these Canons, there are also 'various recent statements of a doctrinal nature that have been endorsed in various ways in the Church of England'.[8] In particular, there are the doctrinal statements contained in ecumenical agreements entered into by the Church of England, such as the Meissen, Porvoo, Fetter Lane

---

8 *An Anglican-Methodist Covenant* (Peterborough and London: Methodist Publishing House/Church House Publishing, 2001), p. 35.

12

and Reuilly Agreements, as well as the Anglican-Methodist Covenant.[9] There is also the statement of the Lambeth Conference of 1888 concerning the Anglican understanding of the requirements for Church unity. The so-called 'Lambeth Quadrilateral' identifies four elements as being necessary for a united Church that would include Anglicans:

1. The Holy Scriptures of the Old and New Testaments, as 'containing all things necessary to salvation', and as being the rule and ultimate standard of faith.
2. The Apostles' Creed, as the baptismal symbol; and the Nicene Creed, as the sufficient statement of the Christian faith.
3. The two sacraments ordained by Christ himself – Baptism and the Supper of the Lord – ministered with unfailing use of Christ's words of institution, and of the elements ordained by him.
4. The historic episcopate, locally adapted in the methods of its administration to the varying needs of the nations and peoples called of God into the unity of his Church.[10]

1.6.4   In addition there are teaching documents commended by the House of Bishops, notably the reports of the Church of England Doctrine Commission together with those produced by the Faith and Order Commission and its predecessor, the Faith and Order Advisory Group.[11] It is relevant to mention two other ecumenical

---

9 *The Meissen Agreement Texts* (London: Council for Christian Unity, 1992); *The Porvoo Common Statement* (London: Council for Christian Unity, 1993); *Anglican-Moravian Conversations* (London: Council for Christian Unity, 1996); *Called to Witness and Service* (London: Church House Publishing, 1999).

10 Roger Coleman (ed.), *Resolutions of the twelve Lambeth Conferences, 1867–1988* (Toronto: Anglican Book Centre, 1992), p.13.

11 Recent reports of the Doctrine Commission include the trilogy: *We believe in God* (London: Church House Publishing, 1987); *We believe in the Holy Spirit* (London: Church House Publishing, 1991); *The Mystery of Salvation* (London: Church House Publishing, 1995); as well as the report on the Christian understanding of personhood, *Being Human* (London: Church House Publishing, 2003). Recent reports of the Faith and Order Advisory Group include: *Apostolicity and Succession* (London: Church House Publishing, 1994); *Bishops in Communion* (London: Church House Publishing, 2000); *The Eucharist: Sacrament of Unity* (London: Church House Publishing, 2001).

statements: the World Council of Churches' convergence statement *Baptism, Eucharist and Ministry* (1982); and the *Final Report* (1982) of the Anglican-Roman Catholic International Commission, which the General Synod recognizes as being consonant with the faith of Anglicans.

1.6.5   Lastly, attention should also be given to *Common Worship*, the series of modern-language liturgical texts authorized by the Church of England from 2000 onwards. While these texts do not have the same degree of authority as the Book of Common Prayer, nevertheless they express the current thinking of the Church of England on the matters which they cover.

1.7 Doctrinal standards: The Methodist Church

1.7.1   The doctrinal standards of the Methodist Church are contained in clause four of the 1932 *Deed of Union*. According to this clause:

> The Methodist Church claims and cherishes its place in the Holy Catholic Church which is the Body of Christ. It rejoices in the inheritance of the apostolic faith and loyally accepts the fundamental principles of the historic creeds and of the Protestant Reformation. It ever remembers that in the providence of God Methodism was raised up to spread scriptural holiness through the land by the proclamation of the evangelical faith and declares its unfaltering resolve to be true to its divinely appointed mission.
>
> The doctrines of the evangelical faith which Methodism has held from the beginning and still holds are based upon the divine revelation recorded in the Holy Scriptures. The Methodist Church acknowledges this revelation as the supreme rule of faith and practice. These evangelical doctrines to which the preachers of the Methodist Church are pledged are contained in Wesley's Notes on the New Testament and the first four volumes of his sermons.

The Notes on the New Testament and the 44 Sermons are not intended to impose a system of formal or speculative theology on Methodist preachers, but to set up standards of preaching and belief which should secure loyalty to the fundamental truths of the gospel of redemption and ensure the continued witness of the Church to the realities of the Christian experience of salvation.[12]

1.7.2　In addition to the *Deed of Union*, the Methodist Church has also produced 'other statements of a doctrinal nature: the *Catechism* of 1986 and the reports on faith and order authorized by the Conference, notably the two volumes (in three parts) of *Statements and Reports of the Methodist Church on Faith and Order* from 1933 to 2000'.[13] Of particular relevance to this present report is the Methodist Conference statement on the Church, *Called to Love and Praise: The Nature of the Christian Church in Methodist Experience and Practice* (1999).

1.7.3　Subordinate to these primary sources are others that contain authoritative statements of Methodist doctrine. The Anglican-Methodist Covenant is one such source. Methodist polity, as expressed in the annual *Constitutional Practice and Discipline of the Methodist Church*, is also an important source of Methodist doctrine concerning the nature of the Church and its ordained ministry. The authorized liturgies found in the *Methodist Worship Book* (1999) express Methodist doctrine, as does Methodism's authorized hymnody, especially the hymns of John and Charles Wesley, which have had 'considerable significance in both shaping and expressing the faith of Methodists'.[14]

---

12 *The Constitutional Practice and Discipline of the Methodist Church*, Vol. 2 (Methodist Conference, 2010), p. 213.

13 *An Anglican-Methodist Covenant*, p. 36. Cf. *Statements of the Methodist Church on Faith and Order 1933–1983* (London: Methodist Publishing House, 1984); *Statements and Reports of the Methodist Church on Faith and Order 1984–2000*, 2 vols (Peterborough: Methodist Publishing House, 2000); *A Catechism of the People Called Methodists* (Methodist Conference, 1986).

14 *An Anglican-Methodist Covenant*, p. 36.

1.8 Theological method adopted in the present report

1.8.1   Comparing these doctrinal standards, it is evident that the primary authority for Anglicans and Methodists is Holy Scripture. In the words of the Anglican-Methodist Covenant: 'Both the Church of England and the Methodist Church ground their belief and teaching on the Holy Scriptures, which they hold to be inspired by God.'[15] However, neither the Anglican nor the Methodist doctrinal standards refer exclusively to Scripture. They also contain references to the Tradition of the universal Church, in particular the early ecumenical councils and historic creeds, and more recent formularies that have their origins in Reformation controversies. In other words, the doctrinal standards refer to an Anglican tradition and a Methodist tradition within the Western Catholic Tradition.

1.8.2   But how are Scripture and Tradition to be used in determining what teaching is consistent with the Anglican and Methodist doctrinal standards? Anglicans apply 'reason' to the reading of Scripture and Tradition, though not in the Enlightenment sense of its being a superior source of knowledge. As applied to the interpretation of Scripture and Tradition, reason refers to the proper use of the renewed mind referred to by St Paul, so that the Church may 'prove what is the will of God, what is good and acceptable and perfect' (Romans 12.2). Reason used in this sense denotes the collective mind of the Church, a community reading of Scripture informed both by Tradition and by the application of critical reflection.

1.8.3   Methodists seek to apply both reason and Christian experience to their reading of Scripture and Tradition. However, in drawing on Christian experience, Methodists do not thereby intend to give theological priority to an individual's subjective view of the world. For Methodists, authentic Christian experience is always experience of Jesus Christ. Such experience does not contradict,

---

15   *An Anglican-Methodist Covenant*, p. 34.

but rather confirms, the truth revealed in the Scriptures, though it may also draw attention to certain aspects of the biblical witness that are in danger of being neglected or overlooked in the life of the Church. An appeal to Christian experience gives explicit recognition to the contemporary world as the context in which the Methodist Church applies its collective mind to the interpretation of Scripture informed by Tradition.

1.8.4   It was the American Methodist theologian Albert Outler who coined the term 'Wesleyan Quadrilateral' to describe the interaction of Scripture, Tradition, reason and experience.[16] Outler did not intend this description to imply the existence of four equally authoritative sources of Methodist doctrine. For Methodists, Scripture remains the primary source of authority, though it is interpreted in the light of Tradition, reason and Christian experience.

1.8.5   The respective theological methods applied by Anglicans and Methodists to the interpretation of their doctrinal standards have a great deal in common, and any differences should not be overstated. When Anglicans apply critical reasoning to the interpretation of Scripture and Tradition they do not thereby reject the role of Christian experience in forming the collective mind of the Church. When Methodists interpret Scripture and Tradition in the light of Christian experience they do not thereby cease to apply critical reasoning.

1.8.6   There is one other aspect of these theological methods to consider. Reference to the 'interpretation' or 'reading' of Scripture

---

16 Albert C. Outler, 'The Wesleyan Quadrilateral – in John Wesley', Thomas C. Oden and Leicester R. Longden (eds), *The Wesleyan Theological Heritage: Essays of Albert C. Outler* (Grand Rapid: Zonderman, 1991), pp. 21–37. Nowadays, Methodist theologians tend to avoid using the term 'Wesleyan Quadrilateral' as it does not adequately convey the complex interaction between Scripture, Tradition, reason and experience.

in the Church can be misleading, inasmuch as it suggests an activity that is primarily intellectual. In fact, reading the Scriptures is a dynamic and interactive process that requires the active participation of the whole community. What constitutes an authentic interpretation of Scripture in the light of Tradition, reason and Christian experience can helpfully be explained using a performance analogy.

1.8.7   A number of recent theologians, including the Methodist theologian Frances Young, have stressed that Scripture is intended to be *performed* in the Church.[17] A musical score is meant to be played; the script of a play is meant to be acted. In a similar way, Scripture is meant not just to be read, but to be performed by individuals in their everyday life and by Christian communities in response to the 'drama' of God's redemptive activity in the world to which Scripture bears authoritative witness. According to the American theologian Kevin Vanhoozer:

> The script exists to tell the church about the drama and solicit its participation. Biblical interpretation is incomplete unless it issues in some kind of performance for, as Calvin says, 'All right knowledge of God is born of obedience.'
>
>   It follows that the most important form our biblical interpretations take is that of lived performance. 'No one can appreciate the full truth of the Christian revelation unless he or she is a player within its distinctive dynamics, participating in the drama of God's self-communication to the world and living out its implications in committed action.'[18]

---

17 See Frances Young, *The Art of Performance: Towards a Theology of Holy Scripture* (London: Darton, Longman and Todd, 1990); Nicholas Lash, *Theology on the way to Emmaus* (London: SCM, 1986), especially Chapter 3, 'Performing the Scriptures'; Kevin Vanhoozer, *The Drama of Doctrine* (Louisville: Westminster John Knox Press, 2005).

18 Kevin J. Vanhoozer, 'A Drama-of-Redemption Model' in Stanley N. Gundry and Gary T. Meadors (eds) *Four Views on Moving Beyond the Bible to Theology* (Grand Rapids: Zondervan, 2009), pp. 160–1.

1.8.8 Because the performance of Scripture takes place in changing cultural and historical situations, which are different from those directly addressed in Scripture, it will always have the character of an improvisation. The Anglican biblical scholar N. T. Wright explains that appropriate improvisation involves freedom and constraint.[19] Such improvisation is not a free-for-all but requires a disciplined attentiveness to past performances. An actor or musician would be unwise to ignore previous performances of a play, or a piece of music, but would be similarly unwise to attempt to re-create them without taking account of the changed context. As well as being recognizable as a performance of the same play or piece of music, a new performance always involves something fresh. In a similar way, the contemporary performance of Scripture in the Church cannot be limited merely to repeating past performances. A *fresh* performance of Scripture is always involved.[20]

1.8.9 The authentic performance of Scripture in the life of the Church must therefore pay attention to several factors: the content of Scripture; the classic performance of Scripture as preserved in Christian Tradition; the world as it is today; and opportunities for improvisation. Thus the performance analogy describes how the dynamic and interactive relationship between Scripture, Tradition, reason and Christian experience enables the Church to live faithfully according to God's will. The doctrinal standards of the Church of England and the Methodist Church are intended to ensure that the performance of Scripture involves a faithful improvisation of what is recognizably the same script, even though a new interpretation is involved.

1.8.10 The theological method adopted by the working party likewise draws on Scripture, Tradition, reason and Christian

---

19 N. T. Wright, *Scripture and the Authority of God* (London: SPCK, 2005). See also Samuel Wells, *Improvisation: The drama of Christian Ethics* (Grand Rapids: Brazos, 2004).

20 See Wright, Ibid, pp.74–7. For the place of Tradition in the performance of Scripture, see Vanhoozer, *The Drama of Doctrine*, Chapters 6–7.

experience in order to discern what a creative and faithful performance of Scripture means for the Church of England and the Methodist Church today so far as the nature of the Church is concerned as a concrete historical reality. The performance analogy allows the Church to be understood as an 'event', though such language needs to be used with caution lest the impression is given that it lacks historical visibility and continuity. The Archbishop of Canterbury helpfully points out that:

> If 'church' is what happens when people encounter the Risen Jesus and commit themselves to sustaining and deepening that encounter in their encounter with each other, there is plenty of theological room for diversity of rhythm and style, so long as we have ways of identifying the same living Christ at the heart of every expression of Christian life in common.[21]

1.8.11   In terms of the theological method outlined above, the working party's task is to state the conditions under which it is possible for Anglicans and Methodists to say with confidence that what actually 'happens' in such circumstances is truly the Church.

1.9 Structure of the report

1.9.1   This report is divided into seven chapters corresponding to the theological method adopted by the working party:

1. Fresh Expressions and the Church
2. Christian Experience: What is meant by fresh expressions
3. Scripture: The Church in the Acts of the Apostles
4. Tradition: The Church in the Anglican and Methodist Traditions
5. Reason: Investigating fresh expressions in relation to the Church

---

21 Foreword *to Mission-Shaped Church*, p. vii.

6. Towards a mission-shaped ecclesiology
7. Conclusions and Recommendations

1.9.2   This first chapter has introduced the task of the working party and the theological method that has been followed in producing the present report.

1.9.3   Chapter 2 describes the origins and principal features of fresh expressions, and includes typical stories of fresh expressions in the Church of England and the Methodist Church.

1.9.4   Chapter 3 investigates the Church in the New Testament, focussing on the Acts of the Apostles as an authoritative witness concerning the earliest Christian communities.

1.9.5   Chapter 4 outlines the subsequent development of a theological understanding of the Church in Christian history, with particular reference to the Church of England and the Methodist Church. The chapter concludes by summarising the current state of ecumenical convergence in understanding the nature of the Church.

1.9.6   Chapter 5 summarizes and assesses the principal criticisms that have been made of fresh expressions and their explicit and implicit theological understanding of the Church.

1.9.7   Drawing on the findings of preceding chapters, Chapter 6 integrates the spiritual and theological insights of fresh expressions with Scripture and the teaching of the Church of England and the Methodist Church concerning the nature of the Church. It defines and describes the principal ecclesial dynamics at work in Christian mission as a contribution to the development of a mission-shaped ecclesiology.

1.9.8   Finally, Chapter 7 sets out the report's summary conclusions and a number of specific recommendations to the General

Synod of the Church of England and the Methodist Conference concerning fresh expressions. While some readers may wish to skip the intervening chapters and turn immediately to the report's recommendations this would be to omit a substantial amount of material that provides the theological basis for statements made in the concluding chapter. The reader is therefore urged to read the whole report in order to understand why the working party has reached its particular conclusions.

2

Christian Experience: What is meant by fresh expressions?

2.1 *Mission-Shaped Church*: Developing a Church of England strategy for mission

2.1.1   The term 'fresh expression of church' (frequently shortened to 'fresh expression') was devised by the working party that produced the Church of England report *Mission-Shaped Church*.[1] It has since come to be widely used in the Church of England, the Methodist Church and in other churches participating in the ecumenical Fresh Expressions initiative.[2]

2.1.2   The working party responsible for *Mission-Shaped Church* was established to produce a successor to an earlier report, *Breaking New Ground: Church Planting in the Church of England* (1994), and with the specific remit to:

• Assess progress with 'church planting' as a mission model;
• Analyse the changing cultural and ecclesial context of mission;
• Provide a perspective on the terminology of 'emerging church' and 'new church';

---

1 *Mission-Shaped Church: church planting and fresh expressions of church in a changing context* (London: Church House Publishing, 2004).
2 Namely, the Congregational Federation, the United Reformed Church and the Ground Level Network.

- Assess typical approaches to church planting and mission, including: youth church; cell church; multiple congregations; network (i.e. non-geographical) church.

2.1.3   The premise of *Mission-Shaped Church* is the conviction that the Church of England is faced with a significant opportunity to review its strategy for mission in the twenty-first century in response to rapid social changes. For the Church of England to be truly the Church for everyone requires an understanding of contemporary culture and a willingness to adapt in response to God's calling. Theologically, this approach is said to exemplify the 'incarnational principle', whereby Jesus was truly among the people of his own day.[3]

2.1.4   *Mission-Shaped Church* asserts that British culture has become progressively detached from its Christian foundations in recent years. During the twentieth century, Sunday school attendance dropped from a peak of 55 per cent to a mere 4 per cent of children with the result that knowledge of the Christian faith among the population as a whole has declined markedly. Although a significant proportion of the population still describe themselves as 'Christian' in the national census, this no longer translates into an identifiable commitment to a worshipping community. Consumerism makes even religion a matter of utilitarian personal choice, while secularisation threatens to banish religion from the public sphere into the realm of private belief.[4] Christendom as a viable concept in Christian mission in Britain has collapsed.

2.1.5   The consequences of all this for the Church of England are profound, according to *Mission-Shaped Church*. Historically, the Church of England has operated with a territorial identity. Present in every local community, the national Church has taken it for granted that the population will request rites of passage at significant junctures in life, and that by such means a sustainable

---

3 *Mission-Shaped Church*, p. 1.
4 *Mission-Shaped Church*, pp. 11–12.

worshipping community will be found in every parish. However, geographical presence alone no longer guarantees that the Church of England can engage with the population. The prevailing culture does not impel the bulk of the population in the direction of their parish church for baptisms, weddings and funerals. It cannot now be assumed that Anglican parish churches will continue to reproduce themselves by traditional means because the pool of people who regard the Church as relevant or important is decreasing with every generation. Now that two or three generations have had little meaningful contact with the Church, a 'come to us' mission strategy that recalls people to faith through participation in worship is no longer viable. The situation in England is not simply post-Christendom: it is a primary missionary situation.[5]

2.1.6   Developing earlier research into patterns of church attendance, *Mission-Shaped Church* describes the population of England (excluding those of other world faiths) as falling into one of four categories: 'non-churched' 40%; 'de-churched' 40% (divided equally between those 'open' or 'closed' to return); 'fringe' attenders 10%; and 'regular' attenders (at least once per month) 10%.[6] Subsequent research published by Tear Fund has brought these statistics up to date: 'non-churched' 34%; 'de-churched' 31% (of whom one sixth are 'open' and five sixths 'closed' to return); 'occasional' attenders 7%; 'fringe' attenders 3%; and 'regular' attenders 14%.[7] While the two sets of statistics are not exactly comparable, the overall picture is clear. The largest group of adults in England are those who have never attended a church of any denomination, except for occasional weddings or funerals. The next largest group used regularly to attend a church at some stage in their life but no

---

5 *Mission-Shaped Church*, pp. 11–12.

6 *Mission-Shaped Church*, pp. 36f. Cf. Philip Richter and Leslie J. Francis, *Gone But Not Forgotten: Church Leaving and Returning* (London: Darton, Longman & Todd, 1998).

7 *Churchgoing in the UK* (Tear Fund, 2007). This report gives statistics for the whole UK. The breakdown of the results into the four nations, and hence the statistics for England, was provided to Bishop Graham Cray.

longer do so. Many of these do not see themselves as open to the possibility of returning to the Church.

2.1.7 *Mission-Shaped Church* also points out the 'time bomb' effect on the Church of England of ageing congregations and declining children's work. It has since been calculated that the average age of Church of England worshippers is 14 years above the average age of the general population.[8]

2.1.8 Not all recent developments are so discouraging, however. There is also good news for the Church of England in the way that Anglicans locally have responded to the challenge posed by changing circumstances. According to *Mission-Shaped Church*, the numerous instances of church plants and similar mission projects during the past twenty years represent the emergence of an alternative approach to mission which is strategically significant and theologically appropriate. Instead of inviting people to 'come to us', this alternative approach seeks to 'go to them'. Endorsing this change of emphasis, *Mission-Shaped Church* argues that the mission strategy of the Church of England should be to develop fresh expressions of church – that is, Christian communities that engage with the situation of contemporary men and women.

2.1.9 As *Mission-Shaped Church* sees it, a necessary pre-condition for moving from a 'come to us' to a 'go to them' mission strategy is an acknowledgement by the Church of England that the parish system is no longer adequate as the sole delivery mechanism for the Church's mission:

It is clear to us that the parochial system remains an essential and central part of the national Church's strategy to deliver incarnational mission. But the existing parochial system alone is no longer able fully to deliver its underlying mission purpose.

---

8 'Celebrating Diversity in the Church of England: National parish congregation diversity monitoring' (General Synod, 2007).

We need to recognize that a variety of integrated missionary approaches is required. A mixed economy of parish churches and network churches will be necessary, in an active partnership across a wider area, perhaps a deanery.[9]

2.1.10 *Mission-Shaped Church* accepts that the development of fresh expressions of church risks putting the diversity-in-unity of the Church of England under considerable strain. However, the report points out that such tension is not unprecedented in the Church. In the New Testament the Gentile mission led to dispute, reconciliation and acceptable diversity within the Church of the apostles.[10] The Fresh Expressions initiative emphasizes that fresh expressions are not intended to replace more traditional forms of church. Nor are the two in competition: in a 'mixed economy' both are required.[11]

2.1.11 A mixed economy should not mean, however, that fresh expressions and traditional churches constitute parallel universes with no interaction and few, if any, features in common. In a mixed economy, properly understood, fresh expressions and traditional churches constitute a complementary and mutually enriching partnership in which each learns from the other. There is sufficient scope within the social context of Christian mission in Britain for both these approaches to be necessary and worthwhile.[12]

2.1.12 The trend towards a 'network society' is identified in *Mission-Shaped Church* as a new factor in the development of an appropriate mission strategy. In Western society a highly mobile population develops meaningful relationships through social networks that depend less and less on geographical limitations of place, such as the neighbourhood in which people live. The significance of this trend for church planting was recognized in *Breaking New Ground*:

---

9 *Mission-Shaped Church*, p. xi.
10 *Mission-Shaped Church*, pp. 97–8.
11 http://www.freshexpressions.org.uk/about/introduction.
12 *Mission-Shaped Church*, p. 96.

'human life is lived in a complex array of networks . . . the neighbourhoods where people reside may hold a very minor loyalty.'[13] Mission based on geographical place and delivered through parishes may no longer be the most appropriate means for the Church to connect with a large proportion of the population for whom their most significant personal relationships are no longer found in the immediate neighbourhood. *Mission-shaped Church* envisages a mission strategy that includes the establishment of 'network churches' for those who identify more with a social network than with a particular place.

2.1.13 *Mission-Shaped Church* therefore proposes a strategy for the Church of England to develop a range of new ways of undertaking mission: some based on parishes; others based on social networks. Such mission initiatives are referred to as 'fresh expressions of church'. The report identifies 12 kinds of fresh expression:

- Alternative worship communities
- Base ecclesial communities
- Café church
- Cell church
- Churches arising out of community initiatives
- Multiple and midweek congregations
- Network focused churches
- School-based and school linked congregations and churches
- 'Seeker' church
- Traditional church plants
- Traditional forms of church inspiring new interest
- Youth congregations.[14]

The list is not exhaustive but illustrates the various kinds of imaginative initiatives that were already being undertaken by some

---

13 *Breaking New Ground*, p. 3.
14 *Mission-Shaped Church*, p. 44.

Anglican churches.15 Subsequently, the Fresh Expressions initiative added two further kinds of fresh expression to this list – fresh expressions focused on children, and those focused on under 5s and their families.

2.1.14 *Mission-Shaped Church* sketches a theological framework for fresh expressions and suggests how these might operate within the Church of England and how they might be resourced and supported.[16] The report also contains several examples of fresh expressions, including mission initiatives sponsored by parishes, deaneries, dioceses, and town centre partnerships. *Mission-Shaped Church* calls for legislation to authorize network-based initiatives but assumes that the majority of fresh expressions will remain parish-based.[17]

2.1.15 In February 2004 the General Synod, on behalf of the Church of England, endorsed *Mission-Shaped Church* and its proposed mission strategy. A number of subsequent measures provide for additional support and resources for the development of fresh expressions. In particular, the Diocesan Pastoral and Mission Measure of 2007 makes provision for Bishops' Mission Orders to allow for the legal establishment of fresh expressions operating across parish, deanery or diocesan boundaries or else in parallel with existing structures.[18] Nevertheless, the majority of fresh expressions in the Church of England continue to be parish-based initiatives. The Church of England has also made provision for the

15 In his speech, presenting *Mission-Shaped Church* to the General Synod, the chairman of the working party said: 'This is primarily a report on what the Church of England is *already* doing in many dioceses, rather than a recommendation that it begin something novel. There is good news to tell, and our recommendations come from a review of actual practice.' Right Revd Graham Cray, address to the General Synod, 10 February 2004.

16 *Mission-Shaped Church*, Chapters 5–8.

17 The related Toyne Report on the revision of the Church of England's Pastoral Measures, *A Measure for Measures* (London: Church House Publishing, 2004) similarly envisages that the majority of fresh expressions will be parish initiatives.

18 For details see http://www.sharetheguide.org/section5/bmo.

selection, training and deployment of pioneer ministers to develop fresh expressions. These are people in whom the Church of England discerns the appropriate gifts and a specific vocation to initiate and develop fresh expressions.[19]

2.2 *Fresh Ways of Being Church*: Developing a Methodist Strategy for Mission

2.2.1   There is much in *Mission-Shaped Church* and its analysis of the current state of the Church of England's mission which resonates with the experience of the Methodist Church. Social trends that have affected the Church of England have similarly affected the Methodist Church. Thus the Methodist Church has found it increasingly difficult to connect with a large proportion of the population through traditional forms of mission. The age profile of the Methodist Church, like that of the Church of England, is significantly higher than the average age of the general population. The erosion of youth and children's work has been particularly serious for Methodism given its former high profile in Methodist mission.

2.2.2   Methodism has consistently held a mission-shaped understanding of the Church, even if this has not always been clearly articulated. Following John Wesley's advice to his itinerant preachers to 'go to those who need you most', Methodists have sought to avoid a 'come to us' approach that expects people simply to conform to patterns of conventional religiosity. A pragmatic approach to mission allows for a rapid response to changing circumstances. Accordingly, British Methodism has been at the forefront of adapting to social and technological developments, though it would be incorrect to suppose that Methodists are any less committed to traditional forms of worship and mission than other Christians. Given Methodism's origins and formative experience as a renewal

---

19 http://www.freshexpressions.org.uk/pioneerministry.

movement in the Church of England in the eighteenth century, Methodists intuitively sympathize with the driving force and aim of fresh expressions. Nevertheless, the ecclesiological implications of fresh expressions are of no less concern to Methodists than they are to Anglicans.

2.2.3   In the course of the nineteenth century the mission of Methodism across all its variant forms settled into a common pattern combining the evangelistic proclamation of the Gospel with an authorized ministry orientated towards the pastoral care of as wide a constituency as could be reached. Methodists have never looked upon themselves as Dissenters or adopted a narrow perspective of a 'gathered church'. Methodists built churches in as many places as possible as a means of engaging with people in their immediate neighbourhood. They provided a variety of worship styles, some of which were similar to those of the Church of England, while others catered for those people who felt little affinity for liturgical forms of worship. Methodism's sense of ecclesial identity and continuity with the historic mission of the Church of England encouraged a generous attitude towards offering rites of passage in the form of baptisms, marriages and funerals, which could be justified as mission opportunities. Methodists invested heavily in Sunday school work, which provided an effective means of engaging with parents and was the most significant source of new church members for most of the twentieth century.

2.2.4   From time to time there have been significant mission initiatives in British Methodism in response to changing circumstances. Most notably, between around 1884 and 1934, the Forward Movement in Wesleyan Methodism led to the building of a number of 'central halls' in city centres, the most famous of which is Westminster Central Hall (opened in 1912).[20] These central halls, architecturally designed and furnished to look like secular concert halls

---

20 See the entry on 'Forward Movement' in John A. Vickers (ed.), *A Dictionary of Methodism in Britain and Ireland* (Peterborough: Epworth, 1999), p. 126.

rather than traditional (and apparently off-putting) church buildings, provided a base for social welfare, evangelistic enterprises and
worship. The large auditorium at the heart of the building provided
a venue for weekday musical concerts and for a form of Sunday
worship in which choirs, community hymn singing and evangelistic preaching were prominent elements. The Forward Movement
arose out of a concern to engage with that substantial section of the
population for whom even the most accommodating of traditional
churches, Methodist or otherwise, held little appeal. A century later,
this same concern is evident in the imaginative way that Methodists
have begun to develop new mission initiatives in the form of church
plants and other kinds of Christian community.

2.2.5   Given all this it is hardly surprising to find that the Methodist
Church, through the decisions of the Conference, has endorsed the
strategy for mission contained in *Mission-Shaped Church*. As has
already been noted (§1.1.4), the *Priorities of the Methodist Church*
include 'Encouraging fresh ways of being Church'. Since 2004 the
Methodist Church has been an equal partner with the Church of
England in the Fresh Expressions initiative. The Methodist Church
report *Changing Church for a Changing World – Fresh ways of
being Church in a Methodist context* (2007) draws on examples of
good practice to encourage the development of fresh expressions
in Methodism. In 2009 the Methodist Church committed itself to
continuing to support the Fresh Expressions initiative for a further
period of five years.

2.2.6   The Methodist Church has also developed VentureFX as a
national initiative specifically intended to develop fresh expressions
among non-churched young adults between the ages of 18 and 35.
This initiative aims to create 20 new Christian communities led
by ordained or lay pioneer ministers to reach out to young adults
with no Christian background.[21] The Methodist Church, like the
Church of England, has made provision for the selection, training

---

21 For details see the *VentureFX* section of the Methodist Church website.

and deployment of ordained and lay pioneer ministers. These are individuals in whom can be discerned the appropriate gifts and a specific vocation to initiate and develop fresh expressions within the Methodist Church.

2.2.7 The Methodist Church does not intend that fresh expressions should replace or compete with local Methodist churches in mission. On the contrary, the Methodist Church is committed to developing a 'mixed economy' in which fresh expressions and local Methodist churches collaborate in mission.

Re:Generation, Romford Methodist Circuit

This church has developed out of the Romford Methodist Circuit's desire to employ a youth worker. The original project has now grown into a recognizable youth church with several young indigenous leaders. Although originally aimed exclusively at a network of young people, it has since become more diverse. It has successfully engaged with non-churched young people, several of whom have become Christians. The pioneers of the project are Ruth and Jamie Poch, Methodist Deacons. Ruth writes:

'I believe the interesting journey we've all had to make has led to deeper discipleship, mainly because we've had to take calculated risks in using young people's talents in a way we might not have done in a more traditional church setting.

It's amazing now to think that the seeds of Re:Generation were sown as a Bible study around our dining room table. Our average Sunday evening attendance is now in the 80s, though 98 recently came through the door which was quite phenomenal.

In early 2010 we organized a survey to find out where people were coming from and we were surprised, in a good way, to discover that many were coming from a non-churched background. It's encouraging to see. We also did a census on the age and the gender breakdown in the church: the average age is 25, and most of those on the 10-strong leadership team are in their early 20s.

Jamie and I are both deacons and our first appointment in 2000 was to the Romford Circuit. We job-shared and our role was to coordinate youth work among 13 Methodist churches which, in some senses, sounded quite a grand scheme; but actually when we got there we discovered that there were very few teenagers involved in the worshipping life of any of the churches.

The work began by listening to the young people and serving their needs. A drama group was set up, social events were organized and monthly youth services began. After a while, the young people were saying, "Look we don't go to any other church, this is our church. We want to have something that we can actually own and have other kinds of activities throughout the week."

Therefore in September 2004 we moved to Gidea Park Methodist Church to 'officially' plant a fresh expression of church among young people. Gidea Park had closed its Sunday evening service, giving us a wonderful opportunity to have that space and time every week.

A core value of the work of *Re:Generation* has been discipleship. Now weekly Bible studies are increasingly led by the young people, and they also have rotas to lead the prayer ministry time and input from Scripture. Our discipleship groups for guys and girls are peer led; so that's very much about going deeper and being able to share things in a safe environment. To have that more intimate setting and the prayer support which comes from that have been key factors in establishing those groups.

At the beginning we prayed for more adult volunteers but it never seemed that God really answered that prayer. In hindsight it has been a blessing because we had to use the young people in the work of the church, or take risks with them serving in ways that we wouldn't have done had we had more mature people coming along at that stage.

Having to take those risks in leadership meant that the young people themselves knew that if they didn't work and do jobs and have vision for the church, it wouldn't work. It all makes for a very exciting journey because it's constantly evolving. When we started, some people thought *Re:Generation* might just meet the needs of the particular group of young people we had at the beginning; but actually, year upon year, we have seen growth – despite key people on the leadership team leaving for university etc.

Interestingly, a few parents began to turn up. I think they were fascinated as to why this church was playing such a big part in the life of their son or daughter. When we ran a *Youth Alpha* course a group of adults started coming to have their own discussion group. Some came on the residential weekend, and it was fascinating and amazing to see how the young people responded as they ministered in prayer and gave support to these adults.

Since then we have had other people coming to *Re:Generation*, some of whom are quite vulnerable with mental health issues and so on. The church has become quite diverse, culturally, and in terms of age range – even though it is still predominantly young people. It keeps us on our toes all the time because we constantly have to cater for an increasing number and a wider age range of people from very different backgrounds.

As pioneers, we found the early years very hard and lonely at times; but if you feel that God has given you a vision to carry on, you persevere and keep on going when it is difficult and try to create an authentic community.

Back in the days of the Bible study in the dining room, we used to ask, "How is everyone doing? Are you having any difficulties?" No-one seemed to have any, and certainly no-one shared what those difficulties were. Now almost the opposite is true. Ask the same question now and you'll begin to wonder if there is anyone who doesn't have some sort of problem going on.

I think that's all because there's now a sense of being safe there, a place where people feel they don't have to wear masks or pretend to be something that they're not.'

Sanctum, Derby Diocese

This story from the diocese of Derby tells how an individual pioneer with a missionary heart for a network of people in an alternative culture developed a fresh expression of church. The fresh expression grew into a mature church that was strong enough to support the pioneer in a new mission initiative in the alternative culture. The pioneer developed as a leader and was ordained by his diocese. He was able to develop indigenous leaders for the maturing church, thus freeing him for further pioneering work.

The story of Sanctum begins with Mark Broomhead, who played in heavy metal bands and had a passion to reach out with the Christian faith to those in alternative communities. He realized that there was a gap between the culture of those in the heavy metal community and the Church which prevented the two from connecting.

So Mark and his band began a bi-monthly worship event using familiar worship songs played in an alternative way. Mark and his team were quick to realize that some people saw these events as 'church'; but he knew these occasions weren't 'church' because they didn't have pastoral elements or a sacramental life: they were just alternative worship events. The team therefore saw a need to plant a new church with a weekly congregation. A local Anglican church, which didn't have a regular evening service, was pleased to let the new church use its building. As this evening congregation grew, Mark and his team shaped it in response to the needs of the congregation. They helped leaders to develop and take responsibility for the church.

A natural partnership developed between the morning and evening congregations so that a new church with a community focus grew from both of the congregations, especially when they moved into a different building. The church continues to grow and support Mark in his pioneering work among those in the heavy metal culture.

Mark reflects that the Church of England is better at supporting churches that fit into the geographical parish structure than creating new churches for alternative cultural groups based on networks. Mark would like to develop a pioneering 'tribal church' for the 'tribe' of people that relate to heavy metal and do not currently relate to the Church in its current form.

The Diocese of Derby has recognized him as a pioneer minister and his church have supported him to begin again to create a new church for a non-churched network.

2.3 Defining fresh expressions

2.3.1   The working party that produced *Mission-Shaped Church* devised the term 'fresh expression of church' in order to convey a sense both of newness of form and continuity of theological content. The term consciously echoes the vocation of the Church of England (set out in the Declaration of Assent) to 'proclaim afresh' the Gospel 'in each generation' (see above, §1.6.2). A fresh expression of church embodies the Gospel afresh in contemporary Christian communities.

2.3.2   The term 'fresh expression of church' was devised in preference to 'emerging church', which label is widely associated with a particular phenomenon in North America.[22] The emerging church movement arose in the latter part of the twentieth century in practical and theological response to the rapidly changing mission context.[23] For the purposes of this present report, fresh expressions of

---

22 The Church of Scotland retains the emerging church vocabulary with reservations; 'Report of the General Assembly of the Church of Scotland' (2009) 3.1/6.

23 The earliest reference to 'emerging church' is William Kalt and Robert Wilkins Henry, *The Emerging Church* (Washington DC: Regnery, 1968). See also, Johann Baptist Metz, *The Emergent Church* (London: Crossroad, 1981). For a general introduction to the subject see Eddie Gibbs and Ryan Bolger, *Emerging Churches* (London: SPCK, 2006).

church are regarded as a separate phenomenon to emerging church (see above, §1.1.6).

2.3.3   As a recently devised term to describe a phenomenon that is dynamic and takes various forms, 'fresh expression of church' is difficult to define in a theologically precise way.[24] Nevertheless, a working definition is needed, if only to avoid the term being used in a way that is inappropriate or misleading. In order to establish their missionary credentials, Anglican parish churches and local Methodist churches might describe a mission initiative as a fresh expression when in reality it is something else. The definition that is currently used by the Fresh Expressions initiative was stated at the outset of this report (§1.1.3). It bears repeating here for emphasis:

- A fresh expression is a form of church for our changing culture established primarily for the benefit of people who are not yet members of any church.
- It will come into being through principles of listening, service, incarnational mission and making disciples.
- It will have the potential to become a mature expression of church shaped by the gospel and the enduring marks of the church and for its cultural context.[25]

2.3.4   The Fresh Expressions website unpacks this definition. A fresh expression of church is not simply a new label for the outreach activities of an existing church or congregation. A fresh expression is a form of church in its own right:

A fresh expression is a church plant or a new congregation. It is not a new way to reach people and add them to an existing congregation. It is not an old outreach with a new name ('rebranded' or 'freshened up'). Nor is it a half-way house, a bridge

---

24 Cf. Steven Croft, 'What counts as a fresh expression of church and who decides?', Louise Nelstrop and Martyn Percy (eds), *Evaluating Fresh Expressions: Explorations in Emerging Church* (Norwich: Canterbury Press, 2008), pp. 3–14.

25 http://www.freshexpressions.org.uk/about/introduction.

project, which people belong to for a while, on their way into Christian faith, before crossing over to 'proper' church. This is proper church![26]

2.3.5   A fresh expression is intentionally 'a form of church for our changing culture' because the Church is shaped by its host environment as well as by the Gospel. While the Church must not be *conformed* to the norms of any human culture, it must be able to *relate* to all cultures in order to be able to transform them.[27] Because fresh expressions seek to relate to different cultures, they have no standard form; nor do they develop according to any single process. To impose a specific form or process of development on fresh expressions would be to ignore their cultural context. Pioneers intending to establish a fresh expression begin by listening to God and to the particular community or network they intend to reach. Accordingly, establishing a fresh expression is more the result of spiritual discernment than strategic planning. Listening leads to finding ways of serving the needs of a community. This is the beginning of 'incarnational mission' within that community.[28]

2.3.6   That fresh expressions can be described as having the 'potential to become mature expressions of church' reflects the fact that they are still 'fledgling' churches or congregations. Attaining a state of 'maturity' does not mean, however, that fresh expressions will then look exactly like traditional churches. They must continue to be able to relate to their cultural context.[29]

2.3.7   The term 'fresh expression of church' is intended to safeguard two central truths concerning the nature of the Church. First, Christ is fully present in each community of his disciples. Second, each community is incomplete in itself without being in a relationship with others. As one missiologist explains:

---

26 http://www.freshexpressions.org.uk/about/introduction.
27 http://www.freshexpressions.org.uk/about/introduction.
28 http://www.freshexpressions.org.uk/about/introduction.
29 http://www.freshexpressions.org.uk/about/introduction.

Only in Christ does completeness, fullness, dwell. None of us can reach Christ's completeness on our own. We need each other's vision to correct, enlarge and focus our own; only together are we complete in Christ.[30]

2.3.8   The creedal mark of 'catholicity' denotes the Church's capacity to embody the way of Christ effectively in each cultural context.

Catholicity refers to the universal scope of the church as a society instituted by God in which all sorts and conditions of humanity, all races, nations and cultures, can find a welcome and a home. Catholicity therefore suggests that the church has the capacity to embrace diverse ways of believing and worshipping, and that this diversity comes about through the 'incarnation' of Christian truth in many different cultural forms which it both critiques and affirms. The catholicity of the church is actually a mandate for cultural hospitality.[31]

2.3.9   The Fresh Expressions initiative has developed its own shorthand notation to sum up the principal features and objectives of fresh expressions:

• Missional – reaching out to non-churched people;
• Contextual – engaging with a particular culture;
• Formational – forming Christian disciples and communities of transformation;
• Ecclesial – becoming new churches or new congregations of existing churches.

2.3.10   The Fresh Expressions 'Share' website provides a classification of the different kinds of fresh expressions. The spectrum of fresh expressions includes:

---

30 Andrew Walls, *The Cross-Cultural Process in Christian History* (London: Continuum, 2002), p. 79.
31 Paul Avis, *The Anglican Understanding of the Church* (London: SPCK, 2000), p. 65; cited in *Mission-Shaped Church*, p. 97.

- *The renewal of an existing congregation* through mission, and especially through careful listening to the non-churchgoers the congregation is called to serve. This might involve radically reshaping the provision of all-age worship, for instance, or rethinking a midweek service.
- *Reinventing an existing 'fringe' group, mission project or community service* so that it is no longer a stepping stone to Sunday church, but becomes 'church' in its own right. A youth group might grow into a youth congregation, or a luncheon club for the elderly might add worship after the meal.
- *Creating a new Christian community within a single parish or circuit*, as a mission initiative. Often it will be lay led and have a relatively small budget. An informal service in a local leisure centre and a midweek after-school meeting for a meal and worship would be two examples.
- *A large mission initiative spanning several parishes or circuits.* It will be more likely to require a full-time paid post and to have a more substantial budget. It could be a new network church across a city centre for Generation X, a town-wide teenage congregation or a home-based church plant on a new housing estate.[32]

2.3.11 *Mission-Shaped Church* suggests five 'values' as 'a broad standard to help discernment' of the principal features of missionary churches.[33] A missionary church is:

- Focused on the Trinity in worship, prayer and mission;
- Incarnational in addressing its specific context;
- Transformational of the community as a sign of God's Kingdom;
- Committed to making disciples who live a Christian lifestyle in a particular culture;

32 http://www.sharetheguide.org/section1/1.
33 *Mission-Shaped Church*, pp. 81f.

• Relational in its dealings with other Christian communities and the wider community.

2.3.12 Although fresh expressions are often regarded as primarily Evangelical in character, in fact they reflect the full range of theology, spirituality and liturgical practice of the sponsoring churches. Thus in the Church of England there are Conservative Evangelical, Charismatic, Liberal and Anglo-Catholic fresh expressions.[34] An equivalent range of fresh expressions can be found within the Methodist Church.

Getting Sorted, Bradford Diocese

In this story a new church that began around one specific area of youth culture – skate boarding – has grown and multiplied far beyond the original small group of young people. It was launched in 2004 by Church Army evangelist Captain Andy Milne and has since been recognized by the diocese through a Bishop's Mission order. Local churches have helped by allowing the use of their buildings. This story is a good example of the mixed economy approach, united in mission to a particular social network that was far from the Church.

As a keen skateboarder, Captain Andy Milne got to know the area's young skaters, many of whom went on to become founder members of the youth church in north Bradford. Now skateboarding is just one of many activities they enjoy every week, as Andy explains:

'We meet on Monday, Tuesday and Friday nights, and we'll see an average of 100 young people during that time. About 25 to 30 get together for the Monday youth congregation from 7.15pm to 9pm; but they are very active and help set up the equipment

---

34 For Catholic forms of fresh expressions see: Steven Croft and Ian Mobsby (eds), *Fresh Expressions in the Sacramental Tradition* (Norwich: Canterbury Press, 2007); and the *Fresh Expressions* DVD 'Sanctus: Fresh Expressions of Church in the sacramental Tradition'.

and run the whole thing really – including worship, teaching, prayer, and activities in between. The age range is 13 to 20.

On Tuesday night, we meet in a different place – at the Salvation Army – and have 5 different groups with anything up to 35 people there. Each group is led by two young people. Sometimes there is a discussion around a Bible passage; and sometimes they work on a fundraising project; but the idea is to try and provide a place where they can really talk about their faith and what they can do with that faith. It's discipleship focused. When they get involved in leadership it really helps their understanding. If they run it themselves, they really own it and the energy triples.

Fridays will see us have a testimony, a short talk for about five minutes, and then different activities in the various rooms. Last year we asked the young people what they wanted to do at this session. We have to be facilitators in it – otherwise they are going to get bored. There's quite a wide age range for this one, it's about 11 to 20, and the older teens run it with some adults as well. We can get 40 or 50 people coming to that.

One room is used for things like live music sessions; there is also a café with a tuck-shop, and games on offer like softball and table tennis. We have people doing 'dj-ing' with mixing and that sort of stuff. It's amazing when you look back to see how things have grown since we were first given use of a *Portakabin* in the grounds of a school. Some of the young people have been coming to us ever since.

What tends to happen is that kids come through their friends or schools to Friday evening sessions because it's very open and accessible to everyone. Then they get to know people, and when there is a bit more trust they tend to move into the other two groups.

When we started, one of the ways I was able to build relationships was through the skateboarding; but it's quite a small part now. It has been good to see a lot of young people come from very different backgrounds to be part of this, and I have been privileged to witness young people having experiences of God on a Monday night, coming to faith and developing into leaders and disciples.

Some local churches realized they hadn't got the resources to do something similar themselves but felt they could support something that's Kingdom-work by allowing us to use their buildings. They show their support for us in practical ways.

We are in the process of setting up *Sorted 2* about a mile-and-a-half up the road because we realized that about 80% of those in *Getting Sorted* were from the same school of around 1,200 pupils. The other school in the area is the sixth largest secondary school in the country with about 1,800 students; but it is currently being extended so will be even bigger. It is multicultural and multiracial.

There was a real sense that God was asking us to go there. One lady dreamt that God was giving us a key to open up something that hadn't been open for some time. People were amazed when we were then invited to go into this school. As a result, we started working with youngsters there and developing groups. We now see about 30 young people every week in *Sorted 2*. It's a massive thing for us.

In the past year, a Church Army team has been drawn together to oversee the whole thing. People from local churches also act as adult volunteers for each *Sorted*, and it all makes a tremendous difference because the work through the schools is growing all the time.

Another exciting development for us is to be granted a Bishop's Mission Order. It means we are now seen as being on an equal footing with other churches, and it also clarifies what *Sorted* is all about in this part of Bradford. The BMO was first mentioned about three years ago when it was noted that *Sorted* is not a seedbed for something else or an extension to another church: it's a church in its own right.

That could clearly be seen earlier this year when six of our teenagers were baptised by the then Bishop of Bradford, Rt Revd David James, in the River Wharfe. A further five then joined them to be confirmed and take holy communion by the side of the river in Ilkley. We find that the young people often have an experience of God before they follow him. Rather than a gradual intellectual process, they often have an encounter with God and begin to make sense of it later.

Going back to where it all started, I have now written a book about skateboarding called *The Skateboarders' Guide to God* in which I try to connect the Gospel with skateboarding mentality and language. I hope to get it published so that it may possibly help others along the way.'

The Welcome, Alderley Edge and Knutsford Methodist Circuit

This story is of a new church growing in a deprived area. It demonstrates the cycle of a fresh expression, starting with Christians listening to a community to discern the needs of the people and then offering loving service to those in the community and finally, after many years, forming an indigenous new church. This church has taken 15 years to grow to its present level of maturity with indigenous leaders who have come to faith and developed within the church. It has been connected to the Methodist Church and supported by the Alderley Edge and Knutsford Circuit. *The Welcome* is now officially recognized as a local church within the circuit. Its minister, the Revd Ben Clowes, tells how the project developed.

'Cheshire is known to be one of the richest and most exclusive areas of the country; but it's a place of extreme contrasts. Around Knutsford we have the Bentley Garage for Manchester, Premier League footballers in £2m homes, charity shops selling *Prada* and *Gucci* – and one of the most deprived wards in East Cheshire.

In the past, the community at Over Ward, Longridge and Shaw Heath missed out on a lot of support and possible grant aid because many charities only look at postcodes when considering applications. As soon as they saw Knutsford, they rejected our application for funding.

Reaching out to the community has always been important at Knutsford Methodist Church and a practice supported across the circuit. *The Welcome* started as one thing and then became something else. The project's first deacon began the work initially by walking around the estate, talking to people, getting to know them – finding out what was needed. The need was for second-hand clothing, so the work of distribution was begun and facilities provided – usually the boot of her car – for people to bring and buy clothes. It moved on from that, and a lease was sought on what was originally a doctor's surgery. This became a Christian place to sell clothing and serve coffee.

By the time the deacon's successor was in post the church began to develop. There had always been a Christian ethos of meeting people where they were; but increasingly the people themselves began to ask why the church was doing this. As the church grew, the community named the place; they were very clear they wanted it to be called *The Welcome*.

In the next phase of leadership a presbyter was appointed and during these three years the church continued to develop and took on a manager, who started to make changes. In time, less clothing was being sold and more coffee was being served. *The Welcome* started to see the growth of an educational project.

The next stage began with the appointment of a presbyter in place of the deacon. A shop was acquired next door to *The Welcome*. This provided space for the café and community use. In 2009 *The Welcome* had a big funding hole but realized that they were giving out such mixed messages when applying for funding. Was *The Welcome* a café, a business, an educational centre and/or a church? A couple of grants were received that helped to keep things going but work with Manchester CiC (Community in Communities) helped *The Welcome* begin a new phase of doing things.

By that stage the church had been meeting for 8 to 10 years. Questions were starting to be asked by the community as to why *The Welcome* was not being officially recognized as a church. It was suggested that the best thing to do was to separate the two elements of the centre – the business side and the church. A not-for-profit company called *The Welcome CIC* (Community Interest Company) runs the refurbished community centre and the café.

The Welcome church was formally recognized as the newest church in Methodism at a special dedication service in September 2010. This was a great month – we had already celebrated the confirmation of two new members. *The Welcome* now had 16 members, and the two most recent additions are dual members – one from Knutsford Methodist Church and the other, our business manager, is an Anglican.

The Revd Dr Keith Davis, Chair of the Manchester and Stockport Methodist District, conducted the dedication service held jointly at *The Welcome* and a local community centre. *The Welcome* style is very hands-on and experiential, and the worship is quite distinct; but in the end, this was quite a traditional service because *The Welcome* members said, "Just because we normally do it differently doesn't mean we can't do it the standard way. We are not fixed to one style like some churches are."

The planning group started to look at liturgies and it seemed to be a contradiction in terms that Methodism was about to celebrate this non-traditional new form of church in a very traditional way. The result was a new form of liturgy, which is available from the Methodist Faith and Order Committee.

The important thing is that this church has come up from the community and is the way this community wants to do 'church' and be recognized as such. Their context and culture is very much concerned for the present moment. At one stage this community was not ready in any shape or form to become a church but things changed. The circuit and local church leadership were ready to help and to react to those changes.

The first time we met as a church there were about 25 of us, and at special services we had more than 100 people. The doors don't open with an expectation that the people will come in: we go to where people are. It has been recognized on the Longridge and Shaw Heath estate that nowhere is as busy or well loved as *The Welcome*.

> The former kitchen supervisor now works alongside the cur-
> rent presbyter in pastoral work. Her story reflects the purpose of
> *The Welcome*. Five years ago, at interview, she said, "I'm very
> happy to do the job of kitchen supervisor, so long as you know
> I don't do God." She is now a preacher in training and senior
> church steward at *The Welcome*. This church continues to be
> a place where God is at work and where people meet with him
> daily. Although we are now a "fully fledged" church and have
> held our first church council (in the style of *The Welcome*), our
> prayer is that we will continue to listen to God and to follow his
> lead as we have done for the past 15 years.'

2.4 Developing fresh expressions

2.4.1   It has proved difficult to establish the precise number of
fresh expressions within the Church of England. A voluntary online register of more than 800 projects was abandoned when it
became clear that in some regions there were actually two or three
times the number of fresh expressions than had chosen to register.
A report to the General Synod based on the 2006 Parish Returns
stated that:

Four in 10 (39%) parishes and churches indicated that since
2000 they had begun a fresh expression of church involving a
new and regular activity. A third (33%) support activities that
involve people who do not currently attend church or who do
so only occasionally. Among parishes that were not actively supporting a fresh expression of church in 2005/6, 2 in 10 (19%)
were involved in plans for the future. That is a further 1 in 8
(12%) of parishes overall making over half (51%) that are supporting or are planning in the next two years to support a fresh
expression of church. Overall 30% of parishes are planning to
begin a fresh expression of church in the next two years.[35]

---

35 'Research towards fresh expressions of church', leaflet for the General Synod
(February 2007).

However, it is not clear whether the question posed for the Parish Returns was sufficiently well understood by recipients for these figures to be considered trustworthy. The question will be posed in a different way from 2011.

2.4.2 The Methodist Church has established a reasonably reliable way of counting fresh expressions. According to the annual Methodist statistics for mission, in 2010 there were around 1,200 fresh expressions within the Methodist Church, which suggests that roughly one in five Methodist churches is involved in developing a fresh expression of some kind.

2.4.3 Whatever the precise number of fresh expressions within the Church of England and the Methodist Church, the reported figures indicate a sizeable phenomenon that has grown rapidly and is present in a wide variety of contexts, urban and rural. If the reported figures from other partner churches in the Fresh Expressions initiative are also included, the total number of fresh expressions in England is even higher. Since the Methodist Church and the United Reformed Church are also present in Scotland, their reported figures include fresh expressions north of the border. Here the Church of Scotland is increasingly involved in developing fresh expressions, and has generated its own theological reflection on the subject.[36]

2.4.4 Thus the horizons of Fresh Expressions now extend throughout the United Kingdom. Fresh Expressions Area Strategy Teams or FEASTs are being developed in more than 30 regions of the United Kingdom. The remit of these teams, ecumenical in composition, is to facilitate the establishment of fresh expressions in a particular area. The teams are made up of a combination of: church leaders (typically, Anglican Bishops, URC Moderators, Methodist

---

36 'Reformed, Reforming, Emerging and Experimenting', a paper written for the General Assembly by Professor John Drane and Dr Olive Drane. An earlier Church of Scotland report 'A Church without Walls' was an important precursor to *Mission-Shaped Church*.

District Chairs); proponents (those who have a vision for fresh expressions); and practitioners, who are currently active in developing fresh expressions. FEASTs seek to promote a mixed economy in which fresh expressions and traditional churches work together in an area. They commission training and provide coaching and mission accompaniment.

2.4.5 Several factors have contributed to the rapid development of fresh expressions throughout the United Kingdom. In practical terms, mission is being approached with considerable creativity and imagination. Fresh expressions are primarily a grassroots phenomenon: a national initiative could not have made such significant progress in a relatively short period of time. Theologically, Christians are thinking innovatively about what it means to be the Church in the twenty-first century.

2.4.6 At a senior leadership level in the Church of England and the Methodist Church there is a willingness to encourage and facilitate mission initiatives, provided always that the integrity of the Church is not compromised. There is an inherent tension in the dual role of church leaders both to encourage mission, which inevitably involves a degree of risk, and to safeguard the integrity of the Church. Accountability is therefore a key issue, practically and theologically, in fresh expressions. Appropriate ways are being devised to support the development of fresh expressions which do not undermine the structures and discipline of the Church. A mechanism for 'provisional recognition' is currently being developed so that fresh expressions of church receive appropriate encouragement and pastoral oversight.

2.4.7 Given the need for accountability in mission, the development of fresh expressions is to some extent 'top down' as well as 'bottom up'. Put another way, the development of fresh expressions involves connecting the 'centre' and the 'edge' of the Church. Diocesan Missioners, District Evangelism Enablers and fresh expressions practitioners work at the 'edge' of the Church in relation to society; whereas church leaders work at the 'centre' of the Church, canonically, liturgically and administratively. Centre and edge can only fulfil their proper role in relation to each other. Thus accountability has a very positive purpose in fresh expressions of church.

2.4.8   Through a combination of imaginative endeavour at the edge and permission from the centre, fresh expressions are developing rapidly in a wide variety of contexts across the United Kingdom. A number of resources are available from the *Fresh Expressions* initiative and partner groups to assist parishes and circuits in developing their mission strategy. Four DVDs have been produced, containing a variety of examples of fresh expressions. Accounts of good practice (including lessons to be learned from failed initiatives) are communicated via the Fresh Expressions website, podcasts and an e-letter. To introduce fresh expressions to as many churches as possible, more than 80 regional Vision Days have been held, involving some 6,000 participants. *Mission-shaped Intro,* an introductory six week course, has been produced for use in parishes and circuits, with an estimated 25,000 participants. The year-long *Mission-shaped Ministry* course, for those intending to start a fresh expression, has been run 61 times, involving more than 2,100 participants.[37] *Mission-shaped Ministry* is governed by a national board and is accredited by a number of universities for the education of pioneer ministers. Numerous presentations about fresh expressions have been made at Diocesan and District synods. Rarely in the life of the Church has a mission strategy been accompanied by such a variety of opportunities and resources for learning and training.

Messy Church, Loughborough Circuit

This story tells how a fresh expression grew from the fringes of a traditional church. So-called 'Messy church' has sprung up in numerous places with considerable success in reaching a

---

37 Statistics as at Easter 2011.

new generation of young families on the fringe of traditional churches.

In 2000 two churches in the Loughborough Methodist Circuit, Knightthorpe and Sileby, began monthly 9.15am services as an experiment. Now 7 out of 10 churches in the circuit run a Messy or Café church. The Revd Jane Carter explains how it happened:

'The 9.15am, half-hour, informal services were for people of all ages. These went well and new people started coming. The service at Knightthorpe was led by a team of lay people, and the service at Sileby, called *Arise*, was led by presbyters. Sileby had coffee afterwards as a "bridge" between the 9.15am regulars and the main congregation. It originally started because of a shortage of people to help at Sunday school. The church had an elderly membership, and this was seen as a new venture. It was something to which we could invite families from the Baptism roll; and we really hoped that it would attract families who were just hanging on at our churches.

The informal services really took off, and one of the interesting sidelines was that a number of teenagers, who had never had any involvement with church at all, began to come along on a regular basis. As a result, we started a youth fellowship.

Following a redevelopment of the Sileby church building, coinciding with the launch of a *Fresh Expressions* DVD describing 'Messy church', the church reviewed what it had been doing and decided to stop the 9.15am service. Quite a few people had said they couldn't come to them because they were too early on a Sunday; so the church re-launched the idea in a different way in the afternoons.

Knightthorpe similarly reviewed its 9.15am service, and with a new presbyter and deacon began a different style of service. Knightthorpe went for a monthly café-style service and Sileby began a Messy church, both starting at 4pm. The format was still very informal with craft, songs, Bible stories, activities, and food. These again attracted new participants.

Other churches in the circuit started to ask about what was happening at Messy church in Sileby. A circuit team was formed, consisting of local preachers and worship leaders to lead Messy church in other churches in the circuit. All our circuit ministers actively support this work.

Now 7 of the 10 churches in the circuit run a monthly Messy church or Café church at 4pm on Sunday afternoons. All have attracted new members. These include both town and rural churches, and one is an Anglican-Methodist Local Ecumenical Partnership.

The issues we are facing now are: How does Messy or Café church help the people who come to grow in their faith? How do we link them into the wider context of the Church, if at all? One church is starting an Emmaus Course and is hoping and praying that members from Messy church will come to this.

We have very good links with local schools. Every month the school at Wymeswold puts an invitation containing the Messy church details into every school bag for the children to take home with them. Messy church is providing a wonderful opportunity for churches to invite those on the fringes. But we need to look at how people can grow in faith and discipleship.

After 11 years in the circuit, one of our presbyters will soon be leaving the circuit; but it's good to see that there are lay people already coming into leadership of Messy church. Around the circuit we are encouraging the appointment of a lay pastor in every church. Three of these lay pastors are already involved in leading Messy church so hopefully the work will continue to grow.

Although numbers are small at the moment, there is real long-term potential for growth and evangelism. Barrow-on-Soar church has dropped its 6pm evening service to concentrate on the 4pm Messy church, and is now getting more people coming at 4pm than came at 6pm.

It has taken time to get things going; but it's very encouraging that a lot of chapels with elderly congregations have seen the vision and gone with it. It's not only young families who are being drawn in: sometimes grandparents bring their grandchildren, and in one area a farmer comes from another village and joins in the activities. Messy church is about participation and contribution. The next steps are to look at the possibility of organizing social events for the parents, as there are lots of opportunities out there.'

Goth Church, Coventry Diocese

This story comes from Coventry City centre and tells how two people worked together to form a church for a network of young people in an alternative culture. The new church grew and developed indigenous leaders. One of the two original leaders has since been recognized and ordained by the diocese as a pioneer minister to grow another fresh expression for a new group of young people in the city centre.

Goth Church in Coventry began when the Coventry Diocesan Youth Officer and the Cathedral youth worker started to walk around the city and discovered a group of Goth young people who regularly congregated in one area. The DYO began to join them just to chat and get to know them; and after a time he thought he would invite them to church and to nearby youth activities. But he soon discovered that they didn't really fit in to church or the other youth activities because they had no concept of 'church'.

The DYO and the Cathedral youth worker got together and decided to run *Youth Alpha* (with pizza!) in the cathedral youth centre for the Goth young people. This was well attended for the first few weeks; but it was soon obvious that, although the Goth young people were enjoying the pizza, they weren't connecting with the course. As the DYO explains, 'We were answering questions that they weren't asking.' The Cathedral youth worker also felt that they weren't listening to what the talks were about. Yet both realized that the young people were responding to the love and respect that they were being given, and that they wanted to be there. Here was a need to develop something different that fitted the culture of the young people and didn't try to 'shoehorn' them into a conventional 'shape of church'.

So, for a while, the DYO and Cathedral youth worker offered space and a listening ear, realising that many of the young people were facing difficult situations at home. At that point, an ordinand from an Anglo-Catholic background came to join them. She noticed that the young people liked poetry, candles and incense. She suggested they try saying Compline at the end of their time together. This simple form of worship was far more culturally accessible to these young people, who responded well. This time developed into a space in which the new community could share and pray for one another. Slowly, over seven years, a church has formed. The original young people are now young adults, and many of them have grown into leadership. Instead of saying Compline, they now end in a time of shared prayer, and there are bi-weekly cell groups called 'Monastree'.

In 2008 the DYO and Cathedral youth worker, noticing a decline in the numbers attending the youth centre, went back into the streets to see where young people were gathering. The police and City Centre Management Company informed them of an area where a group of young people were regularly causing problems through anti-social behaviour. So each week the DYO and the Cathedral youth worker went to see the young people, bringing cans of Coke and taking away prayer requests. Slowly, the conversation developed, and they were able to discuss God and faith with the young people. This went on for ten months; then in the summer of 2009 a barbecue was arranged. Sixty young people came. Many accepted an invitation to the youth centre.

Twelve months later, there are now 500 young people on the books of the youth centre, an eclectic mix of people. The centre is open five nights each week, and the evening always ends with conversation and prayer, for which about half stay.

The DYO is now an ordained pioneer minister, and the diocese is releasing him to grow a church amongst these young people, called 'Urban Hope'. The first gathering of this new church was in March 2011, and 26 young people attended.'

2.5 Theological foundations of fresh expressions

2.5.1   The mission of the Church is primarily to share in the *Missio Dei*, the mission of God the Holy Trinity.[38] Mission is God's activity before it is an activity of the Church. The Church is both the fruit and the agent of the divine mission. Individual Christians participate in the divine mission through their baptism into Christ and by sharing in his threefold office as prophet, priest and king. Consequently, mission belongs to the essence of the Church: it is not just an activity undertaken by some Christians. To share in the mission of God is the fundamental calling of all Christians in all places. Since the Holy Spirit is the leading agent of mission, the Church's mission primarily involves 'seeing what God is doing and joining in'.[39]

2.5.2   The mission of the Church, then, depends upon the activity of the Holy Spirit. The Spirit empowers and directs the Church's mission. The presence of the Holy Spirit guarantees that the Church in any context can receive new inspiration and imagination to engage in mission:

In a world of ever increasing social complexity the church cannot simply adhere to fixed traditional forms. It must reach more and more deeply into its own realities and dynamics within the purposes of God for the world, and invite the Holy Spirit to stir its heart, soul, mind and strength. If it does so, it will learn to participate more fully in the energy of the Spirit of Christ by which God, through his church, is drawing all human society to its fulfillment in the kingdom of God.[40]

---

38 *Mission-Shaped Church*, pp. 84–6.

39 An idea expressed in John V. Taylor, *The Go-Between God: The Holy Spirit and the Christian Mission* (London: SCM, 1972).

40 Daniel Hardy, *Finding the Church* (London: SCM, 2001), p. 4; cited in *Mission-Shaped Church*, p. 86.

Discerning the presence and guidance of the Holy Spirit belongs at the heart of the Church's mission and the development of fresh expressions in particular.[41]

2.5.3   The mission of God in the world is multi-faceted. Drawing on the Five Marks of Mission, as adopted by the Anglican Consultative Council in 1990, *Mission-Shaped Church* and *Fresh Expressions* name the various dimensions of the Church's mission:

- To proclaim the Good News of the Kingdom;
- To teach, baptise and nurture new believers;
- To respond to human need by loving service;
- To seek to transform unjust structures of society;
- To strive to safeguard the integrity of creation and sustain and renew the life of the earth.[42]

2.5.4   *Mission-Shaped Church* adopts the same holistic understanding of mission. In all these dimensions, the missionary task is to proclaim afresh in every generation the faith of the Church, as expressed in the Scriptures and the historic creeds.[43] Since the Scriptures and creeds require interpretation in a changing context, the missionary task further involves a process of inculturation. Thus the report envisages a three-way 'conversation' between the Church as agent of mission, the faith of the Church as expressed in Scripture and the creeds, and the particular culture in which the Gospel is being proclaimed.[44]

2.5.5   The concept of inculturation is central to the mission strategy proposed in *Mission-Shaped Church*. Inculturation denotes the costly crossing of cultural barriers in order to 'plant' the Church

---

41 See Graham Cray, *Discerning leadership: Cooperating with the Go-Between God* (Cambridge: Grove, 2010).

42 *Mission-Shaped Church*, pp. 81 & 99; *Mission-shaped Intro*, Session 1; *Mission-shaped Ministry*, module AO3 'The Mission of God'.

43 *Mission-Shaped Church*, p. 81.

44 *Mission-Shaped Church*, p. 91; cf. p. 100.

in the soil of a different social context. Only in this way does the Church truly replicate itself. 'The Church has to be planted, not cloned.'[45] The theology and practice of inculturation is well established in overseas missions but has received little attention in relation to mission in the West. According to *Mission-Shaped Church*, however, it is a major theological resource in developing the mission strategy of the Church of England.

2.5.6 *Mission-Shaped Church* recognizes that inculturation is susceptible to syncretism, whereby cultural norms blunt the proclamation of the Gospel in ways that effectively challenge and transform society. But the result of failing to take inculturation seriously is that the proclamation of the Gospel becomes irrelevant in that situation.[46] The report identifies consumerism as the dominant ideology of the West and thus the greatest danger as a potential source of syncretism. Responding appropriately to consumerism constitutes the greatest single challenge facing Christian mission in Britain. Regrettably, however, 'The everyday challenge of consumerism is yet to be fully acknowledged by most Christian communities.'[47]

2.5.7 The doctrine of the Incarnation provides a valuable corrective to any possible tendency for inculturation to compromise the integrity of the Gospel. This doctrine affirms that God in Christ uniquely entered the world, taking on a specific cultural identity. Christ's cultural solidarity with the Palestinian communities of his day should be reflected in the Church's cultural solidarity with contemporary communities. This principle has been evident in the Church since apostolic times. The earliest Christian missionaries quickly planted the Church into non-Jewish cultures.[48]

---

45 *Mission-Shaped Church* p. xi; see also pp. 90–1.

46 'In the attempt to be "relevant" one may fall into syncretism, and in the effort to avoid syncretism one may become irrelevant.' Lesslie Newbigin, *Foolishness to the Greeks: the gospel and western culture* (London: SPCK, 1986), p. 7; cited in *Mission-Shaped Church*, p. 91.

47 David Lyon, *Jesus in Disneyland* (Cambridge: Polity Press, 2000), p. 145; cited in *Mission-Shaped Church*, p. 92.

48 *Mission-Shaped Church*, p. 87.

Inculturation based on Christ's incarnation is inherently counter-cultural because it aims at faithful Christian discipleship in the new setting rather than cultural conformity: 'The gospel has to be heard within the culture of the day, but it always has to be heard as a call to appropriate repentance.'[49]

2.5.8   The image of 'planting' the Gospel in the soil of a different culture echoes the parable of the sower (Mark 4.13–20). Jesus used this same image with reference to his own death, which he compared to a grain of wheat falling into the earth (John 12.23–4). Paradoxically, the death of the grain of wheat bears much fruit. The image of 'dying to live' provides a way of understanding the cross-cultural process whereby the Gospel and the Church are translated from one context to another. 'Dying to live' is inherent in the process of planting seeds and therefore provides a model for the Church's mission.[50] 'Dying to live' is sacrificial and counter-cultural. 'A commitment to lay aside one's own preferences, give priority to a different culture, and work with those in it to discover how to express an authentic shared life in Christ, is the opposite of self-centred consumerism.'[51]

2.5.9   *Mission-Shaped Church* does not contain a complete theological account of the Church. Nor does it investigate the ecclesiology of fresh expressions. However, this omission does not indicate indifference among Fresh Expressions practitioners to the ecclesial status of fresh expressions. On the contrary: 'fresh expressions are not "church-lite", but deep church, taking the right shape, in the right place, at a price . . . the comfort and convenience of those who plant them.'[52] *Mission-Shaped Church* affirms that the Church is not incidental to the divine mission but is essentially related to it:

---

49 *Mission-Shaped Church*, pp. xif.
50 *Mission-Shaped Church*, p. 30.
51 *Mission-Shaped Church*, pp. 91f.
52 Presentation by Bishop Graham Cray at the launch of Poole Missional Communities, April 2011.

The Church does more than merely point to a reality beyond itself. By virtue of its participation in the life of God, it is not only a sign and instrument, but also a genuine foretaste of God's Kingdom, called to show forth visibly, in the midst of history, God's final purposes for humankind.[53]

---

53 *Eucharistic Presidency* 2:12; cited in *Mission-Shaped Church*, p. 95.

3

Scripture: The Church in the Acts of the Apostles

Each church is the Church catholic, and not simply a part of it. Each church is the Church catholic, but not the whole of it. Each church fulfils its catholicity when it is in communion with other churches.[1]

3.1 Introduction

3.1.1 The Acts of the Apostles is foundational for all ecclesiologies.[2] It tells the story of the birth of the Church, its expansion from a tiny Jewish sect in Jerusalem to a world-wide mission, its trials and temptations, its successes and its heart-in-mouth near-misses. Acts offers a biblical picture of a Church that is inherently mission-shaped, an *apostolic Church* called and sent to bear costly witness throughout the known world to its risen and ascended Lord. Through the apostolic witness, the Spirit creates a community characterized by *holiness*, a place of encounter with the awesome presence of God. It is a Church whose diversity does not mask its

---

1 From the Porto Alegre statement *Called to be One Church* (Geneva: World Council of Churches, 2006).

2 The exegesis underlying the argument of this chapter is set out more fully in Loveday Alexander, 'What patterns of church and mission are found in the Acts of the Apostles?', Steven Croft (ed.), *Mission-Shaped Questions: defining issues for today's church* (London: Church House publishing, 2008), pp.133–45; *eadem*, 'Community and Canon: Reflections on the Ecclesiology of Acts', in Anatoly A. Alexeev, Christos Karakolis, Ulrich Luz, & Karl-Wilhelm Niebuhr (eds), *Einheit der Kirche im Neuen Testament* (Tübingen: Mohr Siebeck, 2008), pp. 45–78.

underlying *unity*, a Church held together by an overarching commitment to *catholicity*.

3.2 Scripture, history and theology

3.2.1   Luke does not provide a philosophical or propositional theology, a statement of dogma: instead he offers a narrative. Thus studying the ecclesiology of Acts means paying attention to the theology of the Church which emerges from Luke's narrative of the apostolic age. This is not of course the only ecclesiology to be found in the pages of the New Testament: a fuller treatment would need to look at the Gospels and Paul's letters as well as the catholic epistles and the book of Revelation. But the book of Acts holds a pivotal place in New Testament ecclesiology. As the only available *narrative* account of the Church in the New Testament, it provides a unique bridge between the Gospels and the Epistles, a consciously 'catholic' narrative that links the traditions and practices of the Pauline churches with the traditions of Peter, James, and the Jerusalem church. Acts thus offers a unique insight into a transitional and self-reflective phase of New Testament ecclesiology, situated between the variety and vitality of the first decades of the Church's existence and the more ordered patterns that are beginning to develop in the second century.

3.2.2   But how is Luke's narrative to be read theologically? A theological reading involves both paying attention to the theology of the scriptural author and bringing it into conversation with contemporary theological concerns – being attentive, in other words, both to the strangeness of Scripture and to its capacity to speak to the Church down the ages.

> Scripture and tradition require to be read in a way that brings out their strangeness, their non-obvious and non-contemporary qualities, in order that they may be read both freshly and truthfully from one generation to another. They need to be made more difficult before we can accurately grasp their simplicities.

Otherwise we read with eyes not our own and think them through with minds not our own; the 'deposit of faith' does not really come into contact with *ourselves*. And this 'making difficult', this confession that what the gospel says in Scripture and tradition does not instantly and effortlessly make sense, is perhaps one of the fundamental tasks for theology.[3]

3.2.3   Uncovering Luke's theology of the Church is an essential prerequisite to the ongoing theological task, but is not in itself sufficient: contemporary theologians are not engaged in a purely historical investigation. It is impossible in this short chapter to do justice to the wealth of ecclesiological insight that the book of Acts has contributed to the history of the Church (though an awareness of these earlier readings is essential if that history is not to be forgotten). As in *Mission-Shaped Church*, one helpful way to approach the theological task is by mapping the narrative onto the four 'marks' of the church defined in the historic creeds: 'We believe in one, holy, catholic and apostolic Church.'[4] Although this formulation is post-biblical, all four elements are related back to Scripture by the patristic commentators; and they provide a valuable bridge between the historical theologies of the first century and present theological concerns.[5]

3.3 A note on terminology: the *ekklesia* in the Acts of the Apostles

Beside these, the Church in the language of the New Testament always signifies a company of persons professing the Christian faith, but not always in the same latitude. Sometimes it admits of

3 Rowan Williams, *Arius: Heresy and Tradition* (London: Darton Longman and Todd, 1997), p. 236.

4 *Mission-Shaped Church: church planting and fresh expressions of church in a changing context* (London: Church House Publishing, 2004), pp. 96–9.

5 The best guide to the patristic understanding of the four marks of the Church remains John Pearson, *Exposition of the Creed* (1659); revised by Temple Chevallier and Robert Sinker (Cambridge: Cambridge University Press, 1899), pp. 634–60. For a contemporary exposition see *David F Ford, Christian Wisdom: Desiring God and Learning in Love*, Cambridge: CUP. 2007, pp. 258–264.

distinctions and plurality; sometimes it reduces all into conjunction and unity. Sometimes the churches of God are diversified as many; sometimes, as many as they are, they are all comprehended in one.[6]

3.3.1 As Pearson observes, an essential step in understanding Luke's theology of the Church is to pay attention to the words Luke uses for the Church and the way he uses them. Because he is describing the earliest phases of the Church's existence, his language is very fluid: there is no one fixed term for the Christian Church. About half-way through his story, he says that it was in Antioch that the followers of Jesus were first called 'Christians' (Acts 11.28), evidently a nickname used by outsiders to describe a new kind of religious grouping in this pagan Greek city.[7] In Jerusalem, where Luke's story of the Church begins, the followers of Jesus are known as 'Galileans' (2.7) or 'Nazarenes' (24.5). Luke describes them variously as the 'company of believers' (2.44), 'the disciples' (6.1–7, 9.1), the 'saints' or 'holy ones' (9.13), or those who belong to 'what is called the Way' (9.2, 22.4, 24.14). All these terms are indicative of the origins of the Church as a small, sectarian group (a 'fresh expression' of Judaism?) within the broad spectrum of second-temple Jewish pietism, seeking to express its distinctive message in synagogue and temple among a bewildering variety of Jewish ways of believing.[8]

3.3.2 But the dominant term Luke uses for the Church is the word *ekklesia,* which occurs 23 times in Acts, more than in any other book of the New Testament. It is the normal Greek word for a civic or religious 'assembly', and can be used of a Greek city

---

6 Pearson, *Exposition of the Creed*, p. 636.

7 The only other person who uses this title in Acts is the outsider Agrippa (Acts 26.28).

8 For an insightful description of the New Testament Church as a 'fresh expression' of Judaism, see J. D. G. Dunn, 'Is there evidence for fresh expressions of church in the New Testament?', Steven Croft (ed.), *Mission-Shaped Questions: defining issues for today's church* (London: Church House Publishing, 2008), pp. 54–65.

council (as in Acts 19.32–41) or, in Jewish terms, of the assembly of the people of God (as in Acts 7.38 and frequently in the Old Testament). For Luke, the *ekklesia* is most commonly a body of Christian believers in a particular place: the church in Jerusalem (Acts 5.11; 8.1.3; 11.22; 12.1, 5; 15.4, 22), or the church in Antioch (Acts 11.26; 13.1; 14.27; 15.3). So, like St Paul, Luke speaks more readily of 'the churches' (e.g. Acts 15.41; 16.5; cf. 14.23), than of 'the whole church' as a global organization. The closest we get to this global use of 'the church' is at Acts 9.31, where Luke speaks of 'the church in the whole of Judaea and Galilee and Samaria', and at Acts 20.28, where the elders of Ephesus are exhorted to pay attention to 'the whole flock, in which the Holy Spirit has placed you as overseers to pastor the Church of God, which he obtained with his own blood'.

3.3.3   Thus for Luke, as for Paul, 'the Church' is primarily 'the body of God's people in a given place', sometimes meeting in formal assembly, sometimes the body of believers as distinguished from their leaders (Acts 15.4, 22). But the local church is not seen as a (minor) part of a larger organization, but as a locally-grounded instantiation of something bigger which is *the* Church of God. Thus the oddly-marked but significant phrase *ekklesias tēs ousēs* (the Church – that is, the Church as it has its being) in a particular place (in Jerusalem, or in Antioch, or wherever) starts to appear precisely at the point where the Church is becoming geographically extended.[9] In this sense it could be said that 'church' is something that happens when a body of people in a given place start to get together and act together as God's people, under the guidance of God's Spirit. The Church is grounded in the being of God *in a particular place*: it might almost be said, *the* Church is a form of local incarnation of what it means (ontologically, historically, and universally) to be God's people.

---

9 Acts 11.22; 13.1. Paul uses a similar phraseology in some of his letter-openings: cf. Romans 1.7; 1 Corinthians 1.2; 2 Corinthians 1.1; Ephesians 1.1; Philippians 1.1.

3.3.4   The dynamic tension between the metaphysical reality of the *ekklesia* and its local instantiation is seen most clearly at Acts 20.28. When Paul exhorts the Ephesian elders to 'pastor the *ekklesia* of God' he evidently means the *local* flock that is in their charge. But when he adds, 'which he obtained with his own blood', he clearly does not mean that only the Ephesian church has this ontological relationship with the saving effects of Christ's redemption: the whole Church has that relationship (cf. Ephesians 5.25). The flock in Ephesus is a complete and autonomous local expression of what it means to be church – which means, among other things, to be the people of God, redeemed and called into existence by the Paschal sacrifice. What Luke's narrative does *not* provide is a managerial blueprint for precisely how these local instantiations of church relate to each other: and it is precisely in that unclear area that the potential lies for ecclesiological confusion.

3.4 The Church as *apostolic* in the Acts of the Apostles

3.4.1   The central and defining attribute of the Church in the book of Acts is that it is an *apostolic* Church: that is to say, it is a body of people constituted and called into being by the apostolic witness to Christ.

3.4.2   The Church is apostolic because it is sent out

To be an apostle (*apostolos*) is to be 'sent', called and commissioned for a specific task, called to act as delegate or representative of the one who sends. This is where the narrative of Acts begins – with the reprise of the calling and commissioning of the apostles on the Mount of Olives. It is no accident that the Acts of the Apostles starts (in a deliberate overlap with the final chapter of Luke's Gospel) with the risen Lord, gathering together the apostles 'whom he had chosen' (Acts 1.2) and teaching them about the Kingdom of God (1.3). The starting-point and origin of the Church is the group of apostles gathered around Jesus, commissioned to act as his representatives in the world, with the promise of empowerment and authorization from the Holy Spirit: 'You shall receive power when the Holy Spirit is come upon you, and you shall be my witnesses, in Jerusalem and in all Judaea and Samaria, and to the ends of the earth' (1.8). This programmatic statement marks out the Church as 'mission-shaped' from the outset. To be an apostle is to be a witness to the risen Christ, sent out into the farthest corners of the world. Thus the book of Acts offers a centrifugal picture of the earliest days of the Christian Church, starting in Jerusalem and charting the expansion of the Christian community outwards across the Mediterranean world.

3.4.3   This apostolic expansiveness or *extensivity* leads to a Church that is marked by *diversity*: geographical diversity; ethnic diversity; diversity of proclamation; and diversity of liturgical space.

3.4.4   A programme of geographical extension is already built into the programmatic statement of the risen Christ (Acts 1.8). Jesus' promise is fulfilled through the descent of the Spirit upon the disciples on the day of Pentecost (2.1–4), which leads to the proclamation of the Christian message in Jerusalem (2.5–8.1). This proclamation eventually stirs up a great persecution against the Church as a result of which the believers, with the exception of the Apostles, are scattered throughout Judea and Samaria, proclaiming the gospel as they go (8.2–11.18). So, through the preaching of Philip, the gospel reaches Samaria (8.4) and Ethiopia (8.26–38). This same persecution leads indirectly to the foundation of a church in Antioch (11.19–30); and it is this church which (under the guidance of the Holy Spirit) launches Paul on his mission into Cyprus and Asia Minor, up the eastern seaboard of the Mediterranean, and ultimately as far West as Rome (13.1–28, 31). Mission in the book of Acts proceeds by a series of involuntary 'explosions', each one propelling the apostolic witness further afield and creating new church foundations across the Roman empire.

3.4.5   As the apostolic witness spreads across the Mediterranean there is not only geographical expansion but *ethnic diversity*. The first believers are all Jews, but soon the prophecy of Joel that the Spirit will be poured out on all flesh (Joel 2.28/Acts 2.17) is fulfilled. The Spirit sent by the ascended Christ is poured out first on the Samaritans (Acts 8.14–17) and then on the Gentiles, starting with Cornelius and his household (10.1–11.18). The result of this outpouring of the Spirit is the creation of a number of ethnically mixed churches to which both Jews and Gentiles belong on the common basis of repentance, faith, baptism and the gift of the Holy Spirit.

3.4.6   Ethnic diversity is matched by *diversity of proclamation*. In the early chapters of Acts when the Christian message is being proclaimed to those who are Jews or who are familiar with the contents of the Old Testament it is proclaimed as being the fulfilment of the teaching of the Old Testament (Acts 2.14–36; 3.11–26; 7.2–53; 8.26–41; 13.16–47). However, from the story of Cornelius onwards there are also accounts of the preaching of the Gospel in which a knowledge of Old Testament prophecy is not assumed and in which the starting point is either the historical events concerning Jesus of Nazareth (10.34–43) or a basic message about the existence of one creator God as opposed to the many gods of the Greek pantheon (14.14–18; 17.16–31). The basic message is still the same, but the way it is presented differs according to the people to whom it is proclaimed.

3.4.7   The early Church as depicted in Acts also shows an astonishing diversity in terms of *liturgical space*. The first three chapters move from the mountain-top experience of the Ascension to a prayer-meeting in an upstairs room, then out onto the streets of Jerusalem and an unscripted sermon in the temple. But 'this attempt to use the traditional religious space to proclaim the gospel runs immediately into trouble: the wine bursts the old bottles and incurs a hostile reaction (chapters 4, 5). Nevertheless, the unsayable goes on being said, the unstoppable word goes on being spoken – despite everything religious and civil authority can do to stop it – in the public spaces of the temple (5.12–14), in the streets

(5.14–16), and in private homes (4.23). And that essentially is the narrative pattern that Acts is built on, a paradigm that repeat itself in Samaria, on the road to Gaza, in Cornelius' front parlour in Caesarea, by the riverside in Philippi, on the Areopagus in Athens, in prison cells, in workshops, in the School of Tyrannus in Ephesus, in a hired lodging in Rome. Everywhere the word is proclaimed and the Church starts to happen – everywhere *except* (it seems) the conventional religious spaces of temple and synagogue, where the word is contested and finally cast out. And when it is cast out, the word – or rather the Spirit – creates its own religious spaces: not buildings, but communities, small groups practising charitable works (chapters 6, 9, 11), studying the Scriptures and teaching others (chapters 17, 18), working at the ethical implications of their newfound faith (chapters 5, 19) – and sending out their own missionaries (chapters 13–14).'[10]

3.5 The Church as *one* in Acts

3.5.1   But this centrifugal movement, with its built-in impulse towards diversity, is matched from the outset by a centripetal movement towards *intensivity*. Apostolicity is a two-way process: the apostles are sent out in mission, but in following their calling they also provide the growing Church with a constant connection back to its single point of origin. Thus Luke's picture of the Church is marked by a strong emphasis on unity-in-diversity.

3.5.2   Unity of origin
The entire construction of Luke's narrative, starting with the apostles clustered around the departing Jesus on the mount of the Ascension, is designed to show that the whole Church derives its existence from the one Lord, whose teaching and mission command (Luke 24; Acts 1.1–11) power the whole enterprise. The

---

10 Alexander, 'What patterns of church and mission are found in the Acts of the Apostles?', p. 135.

Church takes its origins from the single act of 'sending out' by the one Lord, and the apostolic witness is always a witness to that same Lord. Being with Jesus and witnessing his resurrection is one of the qualifications for being an apostle, as the election of Matthias makes clear (Acts 1.21–22). The diverse apostolic witness, spoken and heard in many tongues (2.1–11), bears constant testimony to the same saving history, the only story Peter knows how to tell (10.36–43). It is a testimony rooted in Scripture and personal experience, differently expressed for diverse audiences, but at the core of all the apostolic preaching in Acts is a remarkably unified presentation of the story of Jesus.

3.5.3 Unity of place

Luke emphasizes the Church's unity of origin in the opening chapters of Acts by focusing the reader's attention on one place, Jerusalem; it's only later the reader learns that the Church (singular) included Galilee as well (Acts 9.31). The unity of the Jerusalem church is constantly underlined through phrases such as: 'all'; 'with one accord' (*homothumadon*; 1.14; 2.46; 4.24; 5.12); 'together' (*epi to auto*; 2.44); and 'one heart and soul' (4.32). The coming of the Spirit at Pentecost happens when they are all together in one place (2.1–4, 4.24–31).

3.5.4 Unity of practice

Peter's Pentecost speech makes a powerful impact on its hearers, and elicits the question: 'Brothers, what should we do?' (Acts 2.37). Peter's response sets out the paradigmatic pattern of Christian initiation: repentance; baptism in the name of Jesus Christ; forgiveness of sins; the gift of the Holy Spirit (2.38). The promise implicit in this pattern is expressly defined as universally extensible, crossing the boundaries of space and time: 'For the promise is to you, and your children, and to those who are far away, every one whom the Lord our God calls to him' (2.39). As the story progresses, the same elements constantly recur, though not always in the same order: baptism continues to be the expected mode of entry into the community, and its mark (whether it comes before or after the rite of initiation) is the gift of the Holy Spirit.

3.5.5 Equally paradigmatic are the so-called *notae ecclesiae* in Acts 2.42, which speaks of the construction of a new fellowship characterized by *intensivity*: that is, focused attentiveness to the teaching of the apostles, the breaking of bread (cf. Luke 22), and the prayers (which, according to Acts 3, implies a measure of continuity with the inherited religious practice of the temple and its daily patterns of worship). Underlying all this is a focus on *koinonia*, on the formation of a fellowship built on the disciples' experience of life together with Jesus, which expresses itself in very practical ways, including the pooling of resources and the relief of want (Acts 2.42–5; 4.32–5).

3.5.6 Unity of mission and ministry

Luke is at pains to stress the diversity of mission and ministry in the early Church. As new churches spring up, new forms of ministry emerge to serve them. Yet his narrative is also structured to stress the continuity between these new forms of ministry and the original apostolic ministry. Thus the Samaritan mission of Philip (Acts 8) is doubly connected back to the apostles, first through their original authorization of Philip's diaconal ministry (6.1–6), then through the apostolic visit of Peter and John to Samaria (8.14–17). Saul, after his conversion on the Damascus road, visits Jerusalem to make contact with the apostles (9.26–30). When the 'scattering' of believers from Jerusalem leads eventually to the foundation of the church in Antioch, the apostles send down Barnabas as their representative to encourage the new church; and Barnabas in turn brings Saul down from Tarsus to ensure continuity of teaching (11.19–26). The Antioch church then provides the launch-pad for the Pauline mission (13.1–3), which soon becomes a mission to the Gentile world (14.46). Even though the ending of Luke's story could not have been predicted from the beginning, there is enough continuity to show that every step in Paul's journey is connected back in some way to the original sending-out of the apostles on the Mount of Olives.

3.5.7 The one and the many

In the second half of Acts the Jerusalem church is no longer the only church: new mission churches are springing up all across the Roman world. So how do the one and the many relate to each other? Where is the Church in Acts? Somewhat surprisingly, the answer is that each church is the *ekklesia* of God instantiated (made manifest, brought to reality) in a particular place (cf. §3.2 above). Rather than depicting the Church as a global organization made up of individual local churches, Luke describes one Church, which has its existence simultaneously in all the particular places in which it exists. Thus each individual church exhibits the same marks of divine calling and redemption, community and holiness that characterized the Jerusalem church at the outset, and that continue to characterize 'the Church of God, which he obtained with his own blood' (Acts 20.28).

3.6 The Church as *holy* in Acts

3.6.1 Holiness is another manifestation of the *intensivity* of the church. Luke does not use the word 'holy' of the church: nevertheless, holiness is deeply embedded in his understanding of what the Church is and what it is for.

3.6.2 The Church is holy because it is constituted by the Holy Spirit

The most frequent use of the word 'holy' in the Acts of the Apostles relates to the Holy Spirit (39 times). Luke structures his narrative in such a way as to leave no doubt that it is the gift of the Spirit which gives birth to the Church and sustains it in its ongoing mission in the world. It is the Holy Spirit who gives power and boldness to the apostolic witness (Acts 1.2, 5, 8; 2.1–4; 2.17, 33; 4.8, 31). It is the Holy Spirit who prepares the way beforehand through the prophets (1.16; 4.25; 28.25). Entry into the community is marked by baptism and the gift of the Spirit (2.38; 9.17; 19.2–6); and it is this same gift that constitutes and validates the reception of the

Word and the growth of the Church (5.32; 8.17; 9.31; 10.44–7; 11.15–16; 13.52; 15.8). It is the Holy Spirit who anoints new believers for particular ministries (6.5; 20.28), and directs them in their mission (8.39; 13.2, 4, 9; 16.6; 20.23; 21.11).

3.6.3   The gift of the Holy Spirit comes from God and is mediated through the passion and resurrection of God's Holy One. Luke has a clear theological understanding of the integral relationship of the Spirit and the Christ-event (Acts 2.33): there can be no pneumatology without Christology. The connection is made explicit later in the narrative: elders are 'appointed by the Holy Spirit . . . to shepherd the Church of God that he obtained with the blood of his own Son' (Acts 20.28).

3.6.4   The Church is an assembly of God's holy people (the 'saints'), formed for the hallowing of God's name. The Pauline term 'saints' (holy ones) is just one of Luke's names for believers (Acts 9.13, 32, 41; 26.10). Luke's understanding of the priestly function of the Church can be glimpsed in his careful re-interpretation of the Old Testament promises to Abraham, minimizing the promise of land and maximizing the aspect of worship (Acts 7.7; cf. Luke 1.17, 74). Thus it comes as no surprise that the ongoing life of the Jerusalem church (Acts 2.42–6) includes a strong eucharistic substratum ('breaking bread from house to house') as well as a strong commitment to traditional religious practices: the practice of prayer, both within the community and within the worship of the temple (cf. 2.42 ('the prayers'); 3.1; 4.23–31; 6.4; 10.9); and the practice of fasting (13.2).

3.6.5   The church is holy because it is a locus of God's presence made active and visible in the world. Hence the importance of 'signs and wonders' in the life of the early Church: a visible extension of Jesus' power over disease, demons, and spiritual rivals (Acts 2.22, 43; 4.30; 5.12; 6.8; 8.9–24; 10.38; 13.6–12; 14.3; 15.12; 19.11–20). The reactions of bystanders and observers to this aspect of the life of the Church are frequently described in terms of 'fear' and 'wonder', appropriate responses to the awesome presence of a holy God (2.42; 5.11–13; 9.31; 14.8–18; 19.17; 28.1–6). Even though there are times when this sense of awe seems counter-productive in terms of mission (5.13), it is still an important aspect of the Church's witness to the living Christ and his presence in his Church (5.14). It is in this context that the puzzling and disturbing story of Ananias and Sapphira (5.1–11) should be understood. The Church carries within its fellowship something of the sacredness of the temple (an idea already familiar to Paul; cf. 1 Corinthians 3.16–17) with the concomitant risk of infringement. The overall effect is to create a picture of a community that is a place of real, powerful, numinous and active holiness, a holiness protected by the Holy Spirit: the apostles are not playing games.[11]

3.6.6   The formation of the holy community

The Church in Acts (as in Paul's letters) is not a community of perfected saints, but it is a community in process of formation marked out by a distinctive lifestyle. Particularly important here are the 'community summaries' (Acts 2.42–7; 4.32–7) that set out the four marks of Christian community: focused attentiveness to the apostolic teaching; to the fellowship (*koinonia*); to the breaking of bread; and to the prayers. Hospitality plays an important part in the development and maintenance of this *koinonia*: both in regular fellowship meals and shared worship (Acts 2.46; cf. 16.15, 40; 20.11); and also in its more intensive outworking in the pooling of financial resources and the practical relief of poverty – something that continued to be an integral aspect of the life of the early Church (6.1; 9.36–9; 11.27–9). It is precisely this *koinonia*, a fellowship that partakes of the holiness of God himself, which falls under the special protection of the Holy Spirit (5.3; cf. Philippians 2.1; 2 Corinthians 13.13). But the practice of hospitality also creates new dilemmas as the Church begins to extend its mission beyond the traditional boundaries of the holy people of God. These

---

11   For the Old Testament background to this story, see Joshua 8.1ff; 2 Maccabees 3; Psalm 105.12–15.

SCRIPTURE

dilemmas are vividly brought to life in Peter's encounter with Cornelius (Acts 10), a complex narrative that issues a dramatic challenge to traditional ways of defining holiness: 'What God has cleansed, you must not call unclean' (10.15). Peter has to learn to allow God to define (or re-define) the boundaries of holiness in ways that may be unexpected: and this painful process of discovery will itself have implications that have to be taken back and worked out in the fellowship of the church (11.1–18).

3.7 The Church as *catholic* in Acts

3.7.1   Equally important in Luke's picture of the Church in Acts is a strong and costly commitment to what the creeds call (though Luke doesn't use the word) the *catholicity* of the church. If catholicity is 'that which is according to the whole', then it could be said (with Pearson) that the Church becomes 'catholic' simply by embracing a wide variety of geographical and cultural settings. But there is more to catholicity than this.

3.7.2   Catholicity and connectivity
The closest Luke comes to using the word 'catholic' (*katholikos*) is at Acts 9.31, where he speaks of 'the church' (singular) in 'the whole of (*kath' holes*) Judea and Samaria and Galilee'. Otherwise (like Paul) he speaks of 'the churches' (*ekklesiai,* plural). The Church in Acts is not so much a monolithic, centrally-run ecclesiastical structure, as a vigorous network of autonomous local congregations, managing their affairs under the leadership of local elders (Acts 14.23; 15.6; 20.17), initiating missionary activity under the guidance of the Spirit, and maintaining links of fellowship and support with other churches (11.29–30). Because Luke sees the Church as a single organic whole he is concerned to emphasize the connectivity that exists within it, especially the connections that link Paul's Gentile mission back to the Jerusalem church. But what he describes is an interactive, multi-dimensional network of connections rather than a centralized, hierarchical system of control.

3.7.3   Catholicity and apostolicity

The key word here is 'network'. Connectivity is built into the system from the start, and the role of the apostles is crucial to the task of keeping the channels of communication open in both directions. In Acts the apostles do not run the local churches. The leadership of the local churches is in the hands of local elders, like the ones Paul chooses and ordains (Acts 14.23; 20.17). But the apostles play an essential role in Luke's economy of the Church. From Acts 8 onwards the apostles (including Paul and Barnabas, though Luke does not call them apostles) have an itinerant 'episcopal' role of engaging in primary mission activity (10.1–48; 13.1–24, 28; 16.1–19, 41) and providing oversight and support for the local churches and their leaders (8.14–17; 9.32–43; 14.21–3; 18.23; 20.17–38). 'The static, centralized authority of the elders in Jerusalem is effectively marginalized in Acts. The autonomous local churches have their own elders, but these are not a central part of Luke's concern. What interests him, and forms the focus of his narrative, is the group that links the two, making the church a loose-knit dynamic network rather than either a centralized hierarchy or a congeries of disconnected congregations. It is the itinerant apostles and their associates, answerable only to the risen Christ and responsive to his Spirit, whose criss-crossing journeys link the local congregations with each other and . . . with their symbolic centre in Jerusalem.'[12]

3.8 Centre meets periphery: the Apostolic Council

3.8.1   All of these strands come together in Luke's account of the first Apostolic Council recorded in Acts 15, a crucial passage for understanding how this connectedness works.

3.8.2   The church in Antioch as a 'fresh expression'

The Antioch church was not founded by the apostles but by anonymous believers from the Jerusalem church fleeing persecution

---

12 Loveday Alexander, 'Mapping Early Christianity', *Interpretation* 57/2 (2003), pp. 163–73 (p. 171f).

(Acts 11.19–21). It exhibits many of the same features of a 'fresh expression' – facing the challenge (and seizing the opportunity) of preaching the Gospel in a different social world, opening up the Word to a new and untouched constituency (11.20), free to develop new forms of leadership, and open to the leading of the Holy Spirit (13.1–3). It is this group that first acquires the nickname 'Christians' (11.26). The initial success of this 'fresh expression' arouses the interest of the Jerusalem church, which sends down a trusted delegate to verify that the integrity of the Gospel is being preserved (11.22–6). Barnabas' mission exemplifies a healthy relationship of trust between the mother church and this new, unpredictable offshoot. Barnabas looks and listens, discerns the grace of God at work, stays to encourage and support – and takes steps to ensure continuity of apostolic teaching in the person of Saul of Tarsus, who is waiting in the wings to discover the mission to which he has been called by the risen Christ. Trust is repaid with trust: far from abandoning the mother church, the fledgling community in Antioch sends a delegation with practical aid when the Jerusalem church is threatened by famine (11.29–30) – a paradigm of connectivity in action.

3.8.3 The boundaries of holiness

But the continued entry of Gentiles into the Church and the success of Paul's mission in Acts 13–14 raise the larger question of what it means to live the Christian life. Should these new converts follow the practice of the Jerusalem church in adhering to the Law of Moses? The first Christians in Jerusalem were observant Jews, and when the Gentiles started to come into the Church it might have seemed obvious to require Gentiles to follow the same practice; i.e. to require circumcision and observance of the Mosaic Law as a qualification for full membership of the Christian community. Certainly, a conservative party in the Jerusalem church thought so; and a group of them travelled down to Antioch to explain their position (Acts 15.1). This sparked a debate within the Antioch church over the status of Gentile believers, and it was the Antioch church that seized the initiative in sending a delegation to

Jerusalem to request a ruling on the dispute (15.2). After a triumphal progress through Syria recounting 'what God is doing among the Gentiles' (15.3), the delegates were received in Jerusalem by three parties acting in concert: 'the church' (i.e. the body of the Jerusalem church); the elders; and the apostles (15.4). Luke makes it clear that it was a small conservative group within that larger body who were seeking to impose purity regulations on the Gentile converts in Antioch (15.5).[13]

3.8.4   The church as a locus for debate

Luke's narrative of the Apostolic Council is revealing. The apostles and elders go into a formal conclave 'to see about this matter' (15.6), which generates 'much debate' (15.7) – a Lucan euphemism for prolonged and inconclusive discussion on a hotly disputed point. This was (as Paul's letters confirm) one of the key points of theological division between Paul and the Jerusalem church, one that threatened to pull the Church apart on more than one occasion.[14] The decisive turning-point in the Council comes when Peter stands up and reminds the assembly of the story he has already told (Acts 11), the story of God's prevenient grace in the conversion of Cornelius: 'And God, who knows the human heart, testified to them by giving them the Holy Spirit, just as he did to us; and in cleansing their hearts by faith he has made no distinction between them and us' (15.8).[15] The initiator of this mission is God, and the apostolic task is to discern God's action in the world and to bring that back to the Church as a primary datum for theological reflection (15.11).

3.8.5   The testimony of Scripture and the testimony of experience

Peter's intervention at this point in proceedings buys silence (Acts 15.12) and allows the assembly, finally, to stop 'disputing' and listen to the experience of Barnabas and Paul – again, testimony to

---

13 See also Acts 11.1–3, where again it is a group within the larger body that raises objections to Peter's meeting with Cornelius.

14 Cf. Paul's account of his controversy with Peter (Galatians 2.1–10).

15 Note how Peter's words echo Gamaliel's concern 'lest you be found to be fighting against God' (Acts 5.39).

what God is doing in the world (15.12). Then it is the turn of the delegates from Antioch to be silent and listen to James, whose primary function in the narrative is to act as an authoritative interpreter of Scripture (15.14–18). Just as Peter was able to link the Pentecost event with the words of Scripture ('This is that which was spoken by the prophet Joel' (2.16)), here it is James who has the spiritual insight and discernment to match the 'this' of God's action in the world (revealed in the testimonies of Peter, Paul and Barnabas) with the scriptural 'that' of God's revelation in the prophet Amos (Acts 15.13). There is a complex process of theological discernment here, a process that begins with the discipline of listening, which requires the ability to move outside the limitations of our own experience to pay attention to what God is doing in the experience of others.

3.8.6 'It seemed good to the Holy Spirit and to us'

James's second role at the Apostolic Council is to express a judgement ('I judge'; Acts 15.19). This is the proper outcome of a civic assembly, meeting in solemn conclave to resolve a dispute which requires some kind of practical resolution (15.19–21). Luke makes it clear that the final resolution (15.22–3) was a formal decision of the whole threefold body (the apostles, the elders and the body of the Jerusalem church). But this decision is not taken alone: the Church acts under the guidance of the Holy Spirit (15.28). In other words, the Spirit is not only active at the margins of the Church – out on the mission field – but at the centre as well. This judgement is expressed in a formal *responsum* delivered to Antioch (and its satellite churches) by four formally-appointed delegates from the Council, two from Jerusalem and two from Antioch (15.22–29). Thus the momentous decision was made that, while Gentile converts should 'abstain from the pollution of idols and from unchastity and from what is strangled and from blood', they need not be circumcised or obey the Mosaic Law in its entirety (15.29). As a result, the Church becomes not only an ethnically mixed community, but also a community with a diversity of religious practice between those who observe the Jewish law and those who do not.

3.8.7 Listening to the margins

This scene plays out many of the tensions between centre and periphery (or between the local churches and the universal Church) which have continued to haunt the Church.[16] The Apostolic Council resists simple description as an attempt to impose centralized control over the church in Antioch. As in Acts 11.2–3, there are those who would like to impose such control; but they do not have the last word. Both Acts 11 and Acts 15 strikingly underline the necessity for the centre to listen to the margins, a necessity embodied in Luke's hermeneutical construction of the apostolic task. It is the role of the apostles (a role fulfilled here not only by Peter but also by James, Paul and Barnabas) to pay disciplined attention to what God is doing in the world, and then to match it up with God's revelation in Scripture. James's ruling is not an imposition on Antioch by the 'circumcision party' but an explicit endorsement of Paul's Gentile mission and of the 'open entry' policy of the Antioch church.[17] This is not a victory for the traditionalists but 'a common platform for engaging difference, allowing both sides to maintain *communitas* while continuing to respect the irreducible diversity of each other's experience of Gospel and Spirit'.[18]

3.8.8 The testing of Tradition

There are two sides to the process of testing the Christian Tradition. The centre has to be prepared to listen to the margins: but the margins also have to be prepared to come back to the centre to tell their story, and to tell it within the framework of the Christian Tradition. There is a necessary aspect of *testing* within this process. As Robert Schreiter puts it:

---

16 For a perceptive and stimulating exploration of the problem in a liberation theology framework, see Robert J. Schreiter, *Constructing Local Theologies* (Maryknoll: Orbis, 1985).

17 Markus Bockmuehl, *Jewish Law in Gentile Churches* (London: T&T Clark, 2000), esp. Chapter 4.

18 Alexander, 'Catholicity and Canon'.

For a local theology to become a Christian local theology, it must have a genuine encounter with the Christian tradition. Any theological formulation can be subject to human failing, to a less than complete fidelity to the message of Jesus. For this reason it needs to be tested against the experience of other Christian communities, both present and past.[19]

But there is also an (equally necessary) component of *testimony* in this process of mutual discernment. 'Just as the tradition is necessary for the development of a local theology, so too local theologies are vital for the development of the tradition. By raising the questions they do, local theologies can remind us of parts of the tradition we have forgotten or chosen to ignore.'[20] In a commentary on Acts written from within the theological turmoil of Latin America, Cuban church historian Justo Gonzalez says: 'The place where we are, at this apparent edge, is where God is doing new things. And those who daily see the new things that God is doing in the world have the obligation toward God and toward the rest of the Christian world to go back to the old centers, which often have lost much of their vision, taking to them our renewed vision of what God is doing today.'[21]

3.8.9   Catholicity in action

This two-fold process can be seen already in Peter's action in Acts 11, when, instead of staying in Caesarea with Cornelius, he takes the risk of coming back to Jerusalem to tell his story – and in doing so to enlarge his own understanding of how the new thing God is doing fits in with the Gospel he has always known (Acts 11.16–17). It can also be seen in the Antioch church's willingness to send a delegation to Jerusalem to test out its own vision by laying the matter before the Apostolic Council, and in the commitment of Paul and Barnabas to make that journey, to tell their story, and to wait

---

19 Schreiter, *Constructing Local Theologies*, p. 34.
20 Schreiter, *Constructing Local Theologies*, p. 34.
21 Justo L. Gonzalez, *Acts: The Gospel of the Spirit* (Maryknoll: Orbis, 2001), pp. 179–80.

for a response. It is seen too in the epistles, which testify to Paul's repeated and costly commitment to keeping the Jerusalem church in touch with his own Gentile churches through the Collection – that very practical expression of *koinonia*, a commitment that was eventually to cost Paul his liberty and probably his life.[22]

3.9 The church in the Acts of the Apostles: some theological implications

3.9.1   So what conclusions follow from all this concerning the nature of the Church in the Acts of the Apostles? What theological resources does Luke's narrative account of the Church offer to help in the construction of a mission-shaped ecclesiology today?

3.9.2   Guided and empowered by the Holy Spirit, the Church demonstrates its *apostolicity* through its faithful response to the commission of the risen Lord. It is *sent out* to bear consistent witness (in a variety of ways depending on the audience) to the God of Israel and God's activity in the life, death, resurrection and ascension of Jesus Christ. An apostolic Church is a mission-shaped Church: apostolicity implies an outward movement, following the leading of the Holy Spirit to bear witness to Christ in a wide variety of geographical settings. Alongside this belong a gradually unfolding inclusivity (learning to share the good news of the Kingdom with all on an equal footing) and a concomitant diversity (cultural and linguistic diversity, diversity of private and public locations, diversity in leadership and worship style).

3.9.3   But apostolicity also entails a process of being 'called out' from the world, of being *gathered* in to be with Jesus and to learn from him (Acts 1.1–3; cf. Mark 3.13–14). Alongside (and logically prior to) the sending out of the apostles is their formation into a learning and worshipping community, sharing table fellowship

---

22   For the collection and Paul's hopes and fears for it, see 2 Corinthians 8–9; Romans 15.25–9.

with their risen Lord and waiting faithfully on the divine promise (Acts 1.4–5). This twofold movement, the *extensity* and *intensivity* of the apostolic life of the Church, entails a strong commitment to the *unity* that underlies and sustains the diversity of the growing Church. The narrative theology of Acts underlines the unity of origin and purpose that lies behind the Church's growing diversity. Luke depicts the Church as an interactive network of local churches, each of which can claim to be an instantiation of *the* Church of God, each with its authentic revelation from God, each operating under the guidance of the Holy Spirit – but none of which can persist in being *the* Church in isolation from the whole.

3.9.4   The inner life of the Church manifests a quality of *holiness* derived from the life-giving gifts and power of the Holy Spirit poured out upon it at Pentecost. The Church is a place of encounter with the awesome presence of God. It is constituted by the Holy Spirit as a worshipping community of faith, discipleship, and service, formed and held together by the apostolic teaching. The Church is the community of those who confess their faith in Jesus Christ as risen Lord and Saviour, recognize his presence in their midst, and respond by leading lives of obedient discipleship, corporately and individually. The Church is the community of those who come to faith in Christ through hearing and receiving the preaching and teaching of the apostles, and who continue to be maintained in their faith by that same preaching and teaching. The Church is a worshipping community constituted by baptism with water in the name of the Father, and the Son and the Holy Spirit (as a visible sign of the Holy Spirit), and by the regular celebration of the Lord's Supper. This community life is expressed in practical ways through mutual concern and charity for one another, especially for the poor, the sick and the vulnerable.

3.9.5   Undergirding all these qualities of the Church, and binding them together, is the mark of *catholicity*. Catholicity is not about centralized control but about 'that which is according to the whole, that in which all have a place'.[23] This catholicity is built on *koinonia*, on the willingness to take the risk of sharing (in both directions) diverse visions and experience of how God acts in the world. In other words, catholicity doesn't just happen: it has to be maintained and fought for, and it comes at a cost. The Church doesn't become 'catholic' simply by expanding in all directions: catholicity only comes with a total commitment to *koinonia*, to connectivity, to keeping the channels of communication open (in both directions) at all costs. Crucial to this connectivity is the apostolic network, which provides the local churches with oversight and support, and ensures their continuity with the Scriptural tradition, and the over-riding task of bearing witness to Christ. The task of the apostles can be seen as a task of discernment based on a triple listening process: listening to what God is doing in the world; listening to the teaching of Jesus (Acts 11.16); and listening to the witness of Scripture (15.16–18).

3.9.6   In sum, the Acts of the Apostles describes a Church that is inherently 'mission-shaped', a Church whose essence is defined from the start by the apostolic commission to bear witness across the known world to the risen Christ. It describes a mission moving steadily outward, responding (eagerly or reluctantly) to the actions of God in the world – a God who is 'no respecter of persons' (Acts 10.34) and whose Spirit is already calling 'those who are far off' (2.39) long before the emissaries of the Gospel have got there. However, this centrifugal programme is only part of the description of the Church presented in Acts, and it would be seriously misleading to stop there. Woven into Luke's narrative account of the Church in the Acts of the Apostles is a strong and costly commitment to the more *intensive* aspects of the life of the Church, traditionally understood under the rubrics of *unity* and *holiness*, held together by an overarching and costly commitment to *catholicity*.

---

23 Justo L. Gonzalez, *The Changing Shape of Church History* (St Louis: Chalice Press, 2002), p. 71.

4

Tradition: The Church in the Anglican and Methodist Traditions

4.1 The Church in Western Catholic Tradition

4.1.1   This chapter sketches the principal developments in the history and theological understanding of the Church in the West since the apostolic period. It follows logically and sequentially from the previous chapter's study of Luke's narrative account of the Church in the Acts of the Apostles. While it is impossible in the space of a few paragraphs to do justice to a long and complex historical process, it is necessary to understand how the Church of England and the Methodist Church have each come to hold their particular theological understanding of the Church, as expressed in their doctrinal standards (cf. above, §1.6; §1.7).

4.1.2   As the primitive Church spread throughout the Roman Empire, it adapted in response to its encounter with the prevailing social and political structures. A significant structural development from the end of the first century onwards was the establishment of a universal threefold order of ministry comprising bishops, presbyters and deacons. This appears to have been in response to the need to safeguard the Church's unity and fidelity to apostolic teaching as the last of the apostles died. The bishop was head of a local church and president of its principal liturgical gatherings, notably the celebration of the Eucharist on each Lord's Day. The communion of local churches was expressed in the communion of the bishops, based on mutual recognition of their ordination into a common ministry. (Thus a new bishop was ordained through prayer and the laying on of hands by at least three bishops of neighbouring churches.) Deacons assisted the bishop by undertaking specific duties relating to worship and service, whereas presbyters were an honorary college of elders advising the bishop. Alongside these three major orders of ministry, a range of minor orders emerged during the course of successive centuries.

4.1.3 Controversy led the principal bishop-theologians of the primitive Church (now commonly referred to as the Church Fathers) to provide the earliest teaching on the subject of the Church. For instance, Cyprian taught that the members of the Church are those who are in communion with a bishop who is himself in communion with the Bishop of Rome.[1] Irenaeus taught that the Holy Spirit is uniquely present in the Church, which possesses the canon of truth in succession to the apostles.[2] Augustine taught that the holiness of the Church derives from God, not from its members, so that the Church is a mixed community of good and bad who will be sifted by God at the end of history.[3]

4.1.4 For the Church Fathers the starting point for theological reflection on the nature of the Church is the salvation achieved by Jesus Christ and conferred by the Holy Spirit according to the eternal plan of God the Father, as revealed in the Scriptures. The Church is a consequence of the paschal mystery of the death and resurrection of Christ and can only be understood theologically in the context of the mission of the Trinity. The Church comprises all those who have been incorporated into the paschal mystery through baptism into Christ's body (or by a desire for such), and

---

1 Cyprian, Epistle LI, *Anti-Nicene Fathers*, Vol. 5 (Edinburgh: T&T Clark, 1990 [1885]), pp. 327–335 (p. 333).

2 Irenaeus, 'Against Heresies', Alexander Roberts & James Donaldson (eds), *Anti-Nicene Fathers*, Vol. 1 (Edinburgh: T&T Clark, 1990 [1885]), pp. 313–567, especially chapter 4, pp. 416–7.

3 St Augustine, *The City of God*, Philip Schaff (ed.), *Nicene and Post-Nicene Fathers*, First Series, Vol. 1 (Edinburgh: T&T Clark, 1994 [1886]), pp. 1–511 (p. 21).

who continue to be sustained by the apostolic teaching and the celebration of the Eucharist. The Church is the visible and effective sign of Christ's reconciling presence in the world.

4.1.5   For practical reasons, in the fourth century the numerical growth and geographical expansion of the Church in many places led to the establishment within the local church of territorial parishes, each with its eucharistic assembly. While the bishop remained head of his church, and thus head of its parishes, he generally appointed individual presbyters to preside at the Eucharist and exercise pastoral responsibility in each parish.

4.1.6   The subsequent development of a monarchical episcopate and hierarchical relations within the Church reflected political structures in the Roman Empire. The bishops of certain churches came to be regarded as metropolitans, while the bishops of the most prominent churches (Rome, Antioch, Constantinople, Alexandria and Jerusalem) became known as Patriarchs. By the fourth century, the Bishop of Rome was commonly accepted among the churches in the West as an authoritative and binding court of appeal in the settlement of disputes, and as the president of councils of bishops. Churches in the East developed their own theological and liturgical traditions. Continuing theological and ecclesiastical disputes between the Church in the West and in the East eventually led to schism in 1054.

4.1.7   The most significant of the early Christian declarations concerning the Church is found in the historic statement of faith known as the Nicene Creed, dating from the Council of Nicaea (325). In this creed Christians profess: 'We believe in one, holy, catholic and apostolic Church.' These four defining marks of the Church were introduced and discussed above in Chapter 3 in relation to the Acts of the Apostles. The marks of apostolicity and catholicity provide the focus of interest in the present chapter, as these have been at the heart of historic disputes concerning the Church itself. Briefly, apostolicity denotes continuity in the mission and faith of the apostles (see above, §3.4). The catholicity of the Church denotes not only its universality but also its fullness and integrity wherever it is concretely found – a mark that entails the connectivity of all manifestations of the Church (see above, §3.7). While Christians today continue to accept the authority of the Nicene Creed as a statement of faith, they disagree as to how these four marks of the Church can be identified and thus also disagree about where the Church is concretely to be found.

4.1.8   Scholastic theologians in the medieval Church in the West came to associate apostolicity with the transmission of ministerial power to successive bishops in an unbroken chain of ministry reaching back to the apostles. This ministerial succession guaranteed that the Church was apostolic. The Church was described primarily in terms of a hierarchy of ministerial power with the Bishop of Rome as Pope at the summit of a pyramid-shaped Church in which the laity formed a passive bottom tier. Counter-Reformation ecclesiology reinforced the authority of the bishops. The First Vatican Council (1869–70) defined the Pope as universal primate and (in certain carefully defined circumstances) as a source of infallible teaching. Roman Catholic teaching on the Church continued to be dominated by scholasticism until the Second Vatican Council (1962–65) introduced a theological sea-change.

4.1.9   The teaching of the Second Vatican Council sets out a fresh understanding of the Church which is biblical, ecumenical and progressive. The one, holy, catholic and apostolic Church is still identified with the Roman Catholic Church but no longer in an exclusive way. While the ministerial hierarchy is maintained, it is now set within the context of a theological understanding of the Church as the people of God. As a living sign of Christ's presence through the power of the Holy Spirit, the Church is said to be the sacrament of salvation. Through its preaching, celebration of the sacraments and authorized ministries, the Church confers the saving grace it contains. The Church is both sign and instrument of the Kingdom of God.

4.2 The Church in Reformation Theology

4.2.1   In the sixteenth century the Church in the West was seriously split following attempts by the continental Reformers to purge it of teaching and practices that, in their view, had no legitimate foundation in the New Testament. Martin Luther identified seven marks of the Church in the New Testament: the presence of the apostolic proclamation of the Word of God; baptism; the Lord's Supper; the administration of discipline (the 'keys'); a publicly authorized ministry; prayer and worship; and self-identification with the cross of Christ through suffering.[4] The resulting break in the transmission of ministry within the first Protestant communities obliged the Reformers to formulate new ways of defining the Church which did not rely on a narrow interpretation of ministerial succession as the guarantee and criterion of apostolicity.

4.2.2   The most enduring of these definitions proved to be that formulated by Philip Melanchthon in the *Augsburg Confession* of 1530. Article VII states that: 'The Church is the congregation of saints, in which the Gospel is rightly taught and the Sacraments are rightly administered.'[5] Despite the reference to saints, this definition does not exclude the unworthy from membership of the Church. Article VIII goes on to say that the visible Church is a mixed body of saints and sinners, and the efficacy of its ministry does not depend upon the moral quality of individual ministers.

4.2.3   The *Augsburg Confession* succinctly states what the Church *is* but does not specify criteria for determining where the Church is concretely located. Nevertheless, the Reformers generally assumed that the 'right' preaching of the Gospel and administration of the sacraments would require an authorized ministry and a teaching

---

4 Luther's teaching on the marks of the Church can be found in his 1539 treatise 'On the Councils and the Church', Eric W. Gritsch (ed.) *Luther's Works*, Vol. 41 'Church and Ministry (3)', (Philadelphia: Fortress Press, 1966).

5 *Augsburg Confession*, Article VII, John H. Leith (ed.) *Creeds of the Churches*, revised edn (Oxford: Blackwell, 1973), p. 70.

authority that are in some sense in continuity with the apostles. Whereas a number of Protestant churches have preserved a three-fold order of ministry, others have instituted alternative patterns. How the Church teaches authoritatively remains an unresolved issue among these churches.

4.2.4   While agreeing with the first generation of Reformers that the Church is to be identified by the proclamation of the Gospel and the celebration of the sacraments, John Calvin emphasized the importance of ecclesiastical discipline. For Calvin, 'as the saving doctrine of Christ is the soul of the church, so does discipline serve as its sinews, though which the members of the body hold together, each in its own place'.[6] Church discipline is therefore a 'bridle' to restrain and tame behaviour, a 'spur' to arouse the indifferent, and a 'rod' to chastise gently those who have 'more seriously lapsed'. Since the Church is the body of Christ, it must not be corrupted by the wickedness of 'foul and decaying members', who should therefore be 'banished from its family'. To Calvin's way of thinking, only the worthy can be permitted to receive the Lord's Supper.

4.2.5   A constant feature of Protestantism has been the unresolved tension between the Augsburg definition of the Church as a mixed community and Calvin's subsequent assertion that the Church is exclusively a community of the morally worthy. Following Calvin's lead, the Puritan tradition within Protestantism was concerned to safeguard the Church's purity by stressing the requirement for its members to be morally worthy. At times the Puritan tradition has been influential within the Church of England and in Methodism, though nowadays it is a minority perspective in both churches.

4.2.6   Despite its ambiguities and limitations, the Augsburg definition of the Church continues to feature in the official teaching of churches that identify themselves to a greater or lesser extent with

---

6 John Calvin, *Institutes of the Christian Religion* (IV, xii, 1), ed. John T. McNeill (Philadelphia: Westminster Press, 1960), p. 1230.

the Reformation. In particular, the Augsburg definition features in the official teaching of both the Church of England and the Methodist Church, to which we now turn our attention.

4.3 The Church in Anglican Tradition

4.3.1   There is no single authorized source that contains a comprehensive statement of the Church of England's official teaching concerning the nature of the Church itself. Nevertheless, the various sources that together constitute its doctrinal standards and official teaching (see Chapter 1) make it possible to piece together a summary of what the Church of England teaches concerning the Church.

4.3.2   A characteristic feature of Anglican ecclesiology is that Anglicans do not consider the Church of England to have its origins in the Reformation in the same way that Protestant churches regard themselves as the product of the reforming process begun by the continental Reformers in the sixteenth century. On the contrary, Anglicans consider the Church of England to be a continuation of the Catholic Church in England, though shaped to a certain degree by the (less radical) English Reformation. Anglicans maintain that the Church of England is '*both* catholic and reformed', and thus stands in unbroken historical continuity with the Church of the apostles.

4.3.3   Its own canons affirm that the Church of England 'belongs to the true and apostolic Church of Christ' (A1). The Preface to the Declaration of Assent likewise affirms that the Church of England 'is part of the One, Holy, Catholic and Apostolic Church' (C15; see above, §1.6.2). The Church of England is not 'the Church' in an exclusive sense but is said to be a church within the one Church.

4.3.4   Article XIX of the Thirty-nine Articles of Religion, entitled 'Of the Church', contains a definition based on that found in the *Augsburg Confession*:

The visible Church of Christ is a congregation of faithful men, in the which the pure Word of God is preached, and the Sacraments be duly ministered according to Christ's ordinance in all those things that of necessity are requisite to the same.

4.3.5   The word 'congregation' is used here in its sixteenth-century sense of meaning a body or collection of the baptised, a sense which includes but is not restricted to a group of Christians gathered for worship. In this sense a Christian denomination would also count as a 'congregation'. The term 'faithful' in this context refers to those who profess the Christian faith, though the Articles of Religion affirm that the Church is a mixed community.[7] Preaching 'the pure Word of God' refers to proclamation and teaching that is based on the witness of Scripture rather than on human traditions and ideas.[8] This does not mean, however, that the English Reformers were opposed to the concept of Tradition as such; rather they believed that only those aspects of the Western Catholic Tradition should be accepted that are in accordance with Scripture.

4.3.6   The same Articles of Religion affirm that the Church of England accepts the two dominical sacraments of baptism and the Lord's Supper. Only these two are properly called sacraments since they alone are 'sure witnesses and effectual signs of grace' instituted by Christ himself 'by the which he doth work invisibly in us, and doth not only quicken, but also strengthen and confirm our Faith in him'. The five other rites 'commonly called sacraments' ('confirmation, penance, orders, matrimony and extreme unction [healing]') are 'not to be counted for Sacraments of the Gospel'.[9]

4.3.7   The preaching of the Word and the administration of the sacraments are said to be marks of the visible Church because through them Christ calls people into a saving relationship with

---

7 Article XXVI, 'Of the Unworthiness of the Ministers'.
8 Article XX, 'Of the Authority of the Church'.
9 Article XXV, 'Of the Sacraments'.

himself and maintains them in that relationship. When the Word is rightly preached and the sacraments are duly administered Christ gathers a community of the faithful around himself and the one, holy, catholic and apostolic Church is made present and visible in that assembly.

4.3.8   Article XXIV 'Of speaking in the Congregation in such a tongue as the people understandeth' requires that preaching and the administration of the sacraments take place in the vernacular because: 'It is a thing plainly repugnant to the Word of God, and the custom of the Primitive Church, to have public Prayer in the Church in a tongue not understood of the people.' The point is made partly to affirm the Church of England's desire to adhere to patristic practice, and partly to express the conviction that unless the words of the service can be understood the people will not be able to make the appropriate response of faith.

4.3.9   The English Reformers decided not only that services should be in the vernacular, but also that there should be one form of 'Common Prayer' used in every church in England. The Church of England today has retained the idea of a nationally authorized pattern of vernacular worship, but now allows greater variation within this pattern so that *Common Worship* with its diverse liturgical forms is authorized for use alongside the Book of Common Prayer.

4.3.10   The definition of the Church in Article XIX makes no explicit reference to ecclesiastical discipline (what Luther referred to as the exercise of the 'power of the keys') as one of the marks of the Church.[10] The most likely explanation for this omission is that

---

10 An example of a definition that includes discipline as a third mark of the Church is that given in the second part of the Homily for Whitsunday in the *Second Book of Homilies* which states that the Church 'hath always three notes or marks, whereby it is known: pure and sound doctrine, the Sacraments ministered according to Christ's holy institution, and the right use of ecclesiastical discipline.' *The Homilies* (Bishopstone: Brynmill Press/Preservation Press, 2006), p. 336.

when Archbishops Cranmer and Parker drew up the Articles of Religion they did not think it necessary to draw attention to what is necessarily implied in the 'due' celebration of the sacraments.[11]

4.3.11   According to this same Article, 'As the Church of Jerusalem, Alexandria, and Antioch, have erred, so also the Church of Rome hath erred, not only in their living and manner of Ceremonies, but also in matters of Faith.' This is a polemical point, intended to explain why the Church of England felt justified in not following Roman teaching and practice. At the same time it rests on a basic theological conviction that because the visible Church is a mixed community of saints and sinners, and because even those who are true Christians are imperfect in holiness and wisdom, the Church in this world will always be subject to error. Yet this error will never be so complete that the visible Church ceases to exist as such in the world (Matthew 16.18); for the Holy Spirit is always at work, leading Christ's followers into all truth (John 16.13). A recent ecumenical text affirms of the Church: 'In spite of the frailty and sinfulness of its members, Christ promises that the powers of destruction will never prevail against it.'[12]

4.3.12   The visible Church, as defined in Article XIX, is neither identical with, nor wholly separate from, the invisible Church. The visible Church can most appropriately be described as the imperfect manifestation in history of the invisible or mystical Church. The sixteenth-century Anglican divine, Richard Hooker, explains that there is no means of discerning the members of the invisible

---

11 Harold Browne, *An Exposition of the Thirty-nine Articles* (London: John W. Parker, 1854), p. 452 states: 'it is probable that the compilers of the Articles, who elsewhere made this use of the keys one note of the Church, omitted it in the Article itself, as considering, that it was implied in the due administration of the Sacraments. For what is the power of the keys and the observance of discipline, but the admission of some to, and the rejection of others from, the Sacraments and blessings of the Church? Where, therefore, the Sacraments are duly administered, there too discipline must exist.'

12 ARCIC, *Church as Communion* (London: Church House Publishing/Catholic Truth Society, 1991), pp.17–18.

Church from among the members of the visible Church.[13] According to Hooker, it is the invisible Church that is the true Church: 'Whatsoever we read in Scripture concerning the endless love and the saving mercy which God showeth towards his Church, the only proper subject thereof is this Church.'[14]

4.3.13 The right preaching of the Word and administration of the sacraments in the Church of England require an authorized ministry. This authorized ministry consists of all those 'ordered' or ordained into one of the three orders of bishops, priests (presbyters) and deacons. The Church of England has traditionally held that these ministerial orders go back to the time of the apostles. As the Preface to the 1662 Ordinal claims : 'It is evident unto all men diligently reading holy Scripture and Authors, that from the Apostles' times there have been these Orders in Christ's Church: Bishops, Priests and Deacons.' The Church of England believes its ordained ministry to be in historical continuity with the apostles and thus an effective sign and instrument of its apostolicity and catholicity.

4.3.14 The *Porvoo Common Statement* explains the particular sense in which Anglicans believe that the ordination or consecration of a bishop in historic succession to the apostles is an effective sign of the Church's apostolicity and catholicity. First, it bears witness to the Church's trust in God's faithfulness to his people and in the promised presence of Christ with his Church. It expresses the Church's intention to be faithful to God's initiative and gift, through living in continuity with the apostolic faith and tradition.

---

13 'The Church of Christ, which we properly term his body mystical, can be but one; neither can that one be sensibly discerned by any man, in as much as the parts thereof are some already in heaven with Christ, and the rest that are on earth (albeit their natural persons be visible) we do not discern under this property, whereby they are truly and infallibly of that body. Only our minds by intellectual conceit are able to apprehend, that such a real body there is, a body mystical, because the mystery of their conjunction is removed altogether from sense.' Richard Hooker, *Of the laws of ecclesiastical polity*, Book III.I.2, R.W. Church (ed.), (Oxford: Clarendon Press, 1905).
14 Hooker, *Of the laws of ecclesiastical polity*, Book III.1.2.

The participation of a group of bishops in the laying on of hands at an episcopal ordination signifies their (and their churches') acceptance of the new bishop and the catholicity of that local church. Such ordination transmits ministerial office and its authority in accordance with God's will and institution. Thereby a bishop receives the sign of divine approval and a permanent commission to lead a particular church in the common faith and apostolic life of all the churches.[15]

4.3.15   The roles of the three orders of ministry in the Church of England are set out in two authorized ordinals – the 1662 Ordinal and *Common Worship Ordination Services*. According to the latter, which is now normally used at ordinations, bishops are called:

to serve and care for the flock of Christ. Mindful of the Good Shepherd, who laid down his life for his sheep, they are to love and pray for those committed to their charge, knowing their people and being known by them. As principal ministers of word and sacrament, stewards of the mysteries of God, they are to preside at the Lord's table and to lead the offering of prayer and praise. They are to feed God's pilgrim people, and so build up the Body of Christ.

They are to baptize and confirm, nurturing God's people in the life of the Spirit and leading them in the way of holiness. They are to discern and foster the gifts of the Spirit in all who follow Christ, commissioning them to minister in his name. They are to preside over the ordination of deacons and priests, and join together in the ordination of bishops.

As chief pastors, it is their duty to share with their fellow presbyters the oversight of the Church, speaking in the name of God

---

15 *Porvoo Common Statement* (London: Council for Christian Unity, 1993), p.26.

and expounding the gospel of salvation. With the Shepherd's love, they are to be merciful, but with firmness; to minister discipline, but with compassion. They are to have a special care for the poor, the outcast and those who are in need. They are to seek out those who are lost and lead them home with rejoicing, declaring the absolution and forgiveness of sins to those who turn to Christ.

Following the example of the prophets and the teaching of the apostles, they are to proclaim the gospel boldly, confront injustice and work for righteousness and peace in all the world.[16]

4.3.16   Likewise, priests are called:

to be servants and shepherds among the people to whom they are sent. With their Bishop and fellow ministers, they are to proclaim the word of the Lord and to watch for the signs of God's new creation. They are to be messengers, watchmen and stewards of the Lord; they are to teach and to admonish, to feed and provide for his family, to search for his children in the wilderness of this world's temptations, and to guide them through its confusions, that they may be saved through Christ for ever. Formed by the word, they are to call their hearers to repentance and to declare in Christ's name the absolution and forgiveness of their sins.

With all God's people, they are to tell the story of God's love. They are to baptize new disciples in the name of the Father, and of the Son, and of the Holy Spirit, and to walk with them in the way of Christ, nurturing them in the faith. They are to unfold the Scriptures, to preach the word in season and out of season, and to declare the mighty acts of God. They are to preside at the Lord's table and lead his people in worship, offering with

---

16 *Common Worship Ordination Services, Study Edition* (London: Church House Publishing, 2007), p. 61.

them a spiritual sacrifice of praise and thanksgiving. They are to bless the people in God's name. They are to resist evil, support the weak, defend the poor, and intercede for all in need. They are to minister to the sick and prepare the dying for their death. Guided by the Spirit, they are to discern and foster the gifts of all God's people, that the whole Church may be built up in unity and faith.[17]

4.3.17 Finally, Deacons are called:

to work with the Bishop and the priests with whom they serve as heralds of Christ's kingdom. They are to proclaim the gospel in word and deed, as agents of God's purposes of love. They are to serve the community in which they are set, bringing to the Church the needs and hopes of all the people. They are to work with their fellow members in searching out the poor and weak, the sick and lonely and those who are oppressed and powerless, reaching into the forgotten corners of the world, that the love of God may be made visible.

Deacons share in the pastoral ministry of the Church and in leading God's people in worship. They preach the word and bring the needs of the world before the Church in intercession. They accompany those searching for faith and bring them to baptism. They assist in administering the sacraments; they distribute communion and minister to the sick and housebound.

Deacons are to seek nourishment from the Scriptures; they are to study them with God's people, that the whole Church may be equipped to live out the gospel in the world. They are to be faithful in prayer, expectant and watchful for the signs of God's presence, as he reveals his kingdom among us.[18]

---

17 *Common Worship Ordination Services*, p. 37.
18 *Common Worship Ordination Services*, p. 15.

4.3.18   In addition to these three orders of ministry there are also various different kinds of authorized lay ministry in the Church of England, including Church Army officers and evangelists. In some cases, such as Readers and licensed pastoral assistants, approved candidates receive authorisation from the diocesan bishop. In other cases, such as worship leaders, candidates are authorized by the parochial church council.

4.3.19   Altogether, the Church of England retains a strong sense of being a territorial church. Its dioceses and parishes extend throughout the whole of England to give complete geographical coverage. Crucially, the parish system of the Church of England ensures that no one is omitted from its pastoral provision. The Anglican parish church and its priest are at the service of all the inhabitants of the parish, maintaining public worship, providing pastoral care and conducting the occasional offices of baptisms, weddings and funerals as required.

4.4 The Church in Methodist Tradition

4.4.1   There is no single authorized source that contains a comprehensive statement of the Methodist Church's official teaching concerning the nature of the Church itself. Nevertheless, the various sources that together constitute the doctrinal standards and official teaching of the Methodist Church of Great Britain (see Chapter 1) make it possible to piece together a summary of what the Methodist Church teaches concerning the Church itself.

4.4.2   While the Methodist understanding of the Church has much in common with that of Anglicans and other Christians, it has three characteristic emphases that are useful to note. First, there is an emphasis on the essential 'connectedness' of local churches, as expressed in what Methodists call 'the connexional principle'. Second, Methodism's societal origins have contributed to creating an emphasis on community, fellowship and mutual accountability – 'watching over one another in love'.[19] Third, there is 'the conviction that the Church should be structured for mission, and able to respond pragmatically, when new needs or opportunities arise'.[20]

4.4.3   'The Methodist Church claims and cherishes its place in the Holy Catholic Church which is the Body of Christ'.[21] The Methodist Church does not claim to be exclusively 'the Church' but to be a particular church within the universal Church. 'The Methodist Church recognizes two sacraments namely baptism and the Lord's Supper as of divine appointment and of perpetual obligation of which it is the privilege and duty of members of the Methodist Church to avail themselves'.[22] Although Methodists do not usually refer to other rites (such as confirmation, marriage, ordination, healing, and reconciliation) as sacraments, they do not thereby deny these are sacramental.

4.4.4   The origins of the Methodist understanding of the Church lie in the writings of John Wesley, particularly his sermon 'On the Church' and his editing of the Church of England's Thirty-nine Articles of Religion. In his adaptation of the 1662 Book of Common Prayer intended for use by Methodists in North America and later in Britain, Wesley retained most of the Articles of Religion, including the first part of Article XIX (renumbered XIII):

The visible Church of Christ is a Congregation of faithful men, in the which the pure Word of God is preached, and the Sacra-

---

19 John Wesley, 'The Nature, Design and General Rules of the United Societies in London, Bristol, Kingswood, and Newcastle upon Tyne (1743)', Rupert E. Davies (ed.), *The Works of John Wesley* Vol. 9 (Nashville: Abingdon Press, 1989), pp. 67–75 (p. 69); cf. Ephesians 4.14–16; Colossians 3.16.

20 *CLP*, §4.7.1.

21 Deed of Union, §4; *Constitutional Practice and Discipline of the Methodist Church*, Vol. 2 (Methodist Conference, 2010), p. 213.

22 Deed of Union, §4.

ments duly administered according to Christ's Ordinance, in all those things that of necessity are requisite to the same.[23]

4.4.5 For Wesley, the Church is found wherever a 'body' of Christians gathers round the preaching of the Word and the celebration of the sacraments, and is committed to scriptural holiness. The Christian life is necessarily corporate and thus ecclesial: there can be 'no holiness but social holiness' since 'the Bible knows nothing of solitary religion'.[24] 'The Catholic or universal church is all the persons in the universe whom God hath so called out of the world as to entitle them to the preceding character [of holiness]; as to be "one body", united by "one spirit"; having "one faith, one hope, one baptism; one God and Father of all, who is above all, and through all, and in them all".'[25] Being committed to a generous interpretation of what it means for 'the pure Word of God' to be preached and the sacraments to be 'duly administered', Wesley was reluctant to 'unchurch' other Christians – a trait that continues to be characteristic of Methodism today.

4.4.6 Besides the writings of John Wesley, Methodism's understanding of the Church has also been influenced by its history as a renewal movement. At first, John and Charles Wesley's network or connexion of Methodist societies constituted a movement within the Church of England at the service of mission, interpreted as the proclamation of the evangelical faith and the spread of scriptural holiness. Since the Methodist economy was auxiliary to that of the Church of England (being intended to reform church and nation), Methodism was not 'the Church'. The Wesley brothers expected Methodists to attend Sunday worship in their Anglican

---

23 James F. White (ed.), *John Wesley's Prayer Book: The Sunday Service of the Methodists in North America* (Akron, Ohio: OSL Publications, 1991), p. 310.

24 Preface to 'Hymns and Sacred Poems' (1739); *The Works of the Rev. John Wesley* Vol. 14 (London: Methodist Conference, 1856), pp. 303–6 (p. 305); John Telford, *The Life of John Wesley*, 4th edn (London: Epworth, 1924 [1906]), p. 147.

25 Sermon 74 'Of the Church', Albert C. Outler (ed.), *The Works of John Wesley* Vol. 3 (Nashville: Abingdon, 1986), pp. 45–57 (p. 50).

parish church, where they would also receive the sacraments. To avoid competition, John and Charles would not permit Methodist preaching services and other activities to be held during 'church hours'. Despite frequent calls from some of the itinerant Methodist preachers for separation from the Church of England, John continued to hope that the Methodist societies would remain within the national church. Charles fiercely opposed separation from the Church of England. The elderly John Wesley, however, regarding himself as apostle to the Methodists, and convinced from his reading of Anglican divines that 'bishops and presbyters are essentially of the same order', took it upon himself in the face of an acute shortage of Anglican priests in North America to provide an ordained ministry for Methodism in the United States.[26] While his precise intention in laying hands on Thomas Coke for superintendency in America is still debated, this action proved decisive in turning Methodism in the United States *de facto* into a church.

4.4.7 John Wesley's intended pattern of ministry for the Methodist societies was never implemented in Britain, though there were a few ordinations prior to his death in 1791. The rejection of the Lichfield Plan (1794), which proposed a threefold ministry of superintendent, elder and deacon, left the itinerant preachers (regarded by Wesley as extra-ordinary messengers of the Gospel) to become, in effect, a single order of ministry for the Methodist societies, which now faced the future without internal pressure to

---

26 'Journal of John Wesley', 20 January 1746; W. Reginald Ward and Richard P. Heitzenrater (eds), *The Works of John Wesley*, Vol. 20 (Nashville: Abingdon, 1991), p. 112. The most influential Anglican divines on Wesley in this regard were Lord Peter King and Edward Stillingfleet. Cf. Baron Peter King, *An Inquiry into the Constitutions, Discipline, Unity and Worship of the Primitive Church* (London, 1691); Edward Stillingfleet, *Irenicum, A weapon-salve for the churches wounds. Or, the divine right of particular forms of church-government* (London, 1661). 'To his brother Charles' on 8 June 1780, Wesley wrote: 'Read Bishop Stillingfleet's *Irenicon* or any impartial history of the Ancient Church, and I believe you will think as I do. I verily believe I have as good a right to ordain as to administer the Lord's Supper. But I see abundance of reasons why I should not use that right, unless I was turned out of the Church.' John Telford (ed.), *The Letters of the Rev. John Wesley A.M* Vol. 7 (London: Epworth, 1931), p. 21. By 1784 Wesley had overcome any scruples about ordaining others.

keep them within the Church of England. Under the Plan of Pacifi-
cation (1795), the Methodist societies in Britain became ecclesially
self-sufficient under their itinerant preachers, who assimilated the
status and functions of an ordained ministry, preaching the Gospel
and administering the sacraments of baptism and the Lord's Supper. Thus, somewhat untidily and without ever formally separat-
ing from the Church of England, Methodism in Britain became *de
facto* a church, albeit one that soon split into various competing
denominations until finally brought together again in 1932.

4.4.8   The first Methodist teaching document specifically on the
Church, *The Nature of the Christian Church* (1937), defines the
Church in a way that is consistent with John Wesley's Articles of
Religion: 'The Church of Christ on earth is a redeemed society of
believers, whose duty and privilege it is to share in the gift of the
Holy Spirit, and to enjoy that communion with God the Father
which has been granted in the forgiveness of sins through our Lord
Jesus Christ.'[27] The visible Church is easily identified: 'the Church
of Christ on earth means all the believers, in whatever community
they are found, who confess Jesus as Lord, to the glory of God the
Father'. The marks of the visible Church are:

> the possession and acknowledgement of the Word of God as
> given in Scripture, and as interpreted by the Holy Spirit to the
> Church and to the individual; the profession of faith in God as
> he is incarnate and revealed in Christ; the observance of the Sac-
> raments of Baptism and the Lord's Supper; and a ministry for the
> pastoral office, the preaching of the Word and the administra-
> tion of the Sacraments.[28]

4.4.9   On this basis, the apostolicity of Methodism consists in
continuity of: Christian experience; fellowship in the Holy Spirit;

---

27 *The Nature of the Christian Church*, in *Statements of the Methodist Church on
Faith and Order 1933–1983* (Methodist Conference, 1984), pp. 5–42 [hereafter NCC],
p. 40.
28 NCC, p. 41.

allegiance to one Lord; proclamation of the Gospel; and mission. For Methodists, the 'doctrine of apostolic succession' means the succession of believers, a 'long chain' stretching back to the first disciples.[29] The continuity of the Church does not depend upon, nor is it necessarily secured by, ministerial succession. Despite the existence of sin and error in the Church, the proclamation of the Word and the celebration of the sacraments 'have never been wholly without power'.[30]

4.4.10 *Called to Love and Praise* updates for a new context (but does not contradict) the teaching of the 1937 statement. The framework for Methodist theological reflection concerning the Church is the doctrine of the Trinity: 'God's reign and mission, focussed and expressed supremely in the revelation of God as Father, Son and Holy Spirit, are the foundation of any authentically Christian understanding of the Church'.[31] The relationship between the Church and the Kingdom of God is precisely defined: 'As agent of God's mission, the Church is a sign, foretaste and instrument of the kingdom.'[32]

4.4.11 *Called to Love and Praise* envisages (but does not actually endorse) a radical interpretation of the Augsburg definition of the Church found in John Wesley's Articles of Religion and subsequent Methodist teaching: 'There is something to be said for a specific, but less tightly drawn criterion: wherever people join together to respond to Christ as Lord – there is the Church.'[33] This radical interpretation is said to be consistent with the fact that Methodists 'have generally been reluctant to unchurch any body of professedly Christian believers, even where they may lack certain elements – for example, the celebration of the two gospel sacraments – which

---

29 *NCC*, p. 32.
30 *NCC*, p. 33.
31 *CLP*, §2.1.12.
32 *CLP*, §1.4.1.
33 *CLP*, §2.4.9.

Methodists consider as normative for the Church'.[34] It should be noted that Methodists continue to affirm that certain ecclesial elements are normative of the Church. Moreover, the connexional principle ensures that joining together to respond to Christ as Lord involves being visibly joined with other such communities.

4.4.12   Concerning the scope and content of the apostolic tradition, *Called to Love and Praise* affirms the 'ecumenical consensus' that:

> apostolic tradition in the Church means continuity in the permanent characteristics of the Church of the apostles: witness to the apostolic faith, proclamation and fresh interpretation of the Gospel, celebration of baptism and the Eucharist, the transmission of ministerial responsibilities, communion in prayer, love, joy and suffering, service to the sick and the needy, unity among the local churches and sharing the gifts which the Lord has given to each. (*BEM* M34).[35]

4.4.13   Although John Wesley intended Methodists to use his adaptation of the 1662 Book of Common Prayer, he introduced two innovations into the liturgy – hymns and extempore prayer – which later proved significant for the development of Methodist worship. As a result, the principal form of Methodist worship became the preaching service in which hymn singing and extempore prayer featured prominently. Today, Methodist worship continues to reflect these contrasting historical influences. The *Methodist Worship Book* (1999) contains authorized liturgies for use in Methodist worship. According to the Preface, however, '"These forms are not intended to curb creative freedom, but rather to provide norms for its guidance." Within our heritage, both fixed forms and freer expressions of worship have been, and should continue to be, valued' (p. viii).

---

34 *CLP*, §2.4.9.
35 *CLP*, §2.4.7.

4.4.14   Methodists consider a 'connexional' polity to be part of the apostolic tradition and therefore normative for the Church. Local churches are interdependent, bound to one another through visible structures of communion or *koinonia*, which include structures of oversight, governance and fellowship. Only by being in 'connexion' with others can a local church truly be the universal Church, exercising the whole ministry of Christ. Accordingly, the *Constitutional Practice and Discipline of the Methodist Church* defines the local church as a worshipping 'congregation' that is always connected with others in a circuit. 'The Church exists to exercise the whole ministry of Christ. The Local Church, with its membership and larger church community, exercises this ministry where it is and shares in the wider ministry of the Church in the world.'[36]

4.4.15   The transmission of ordained ministry under the corporate oversight of the Methodist Conference also belongs to the apostolic tradition of ministerial succession. The *Methodist Worship Book* (1999) provides a convenient summary of Methodist teaching concerning the ordained ministry:

> The Methodist Church has received and transmitted two orders of ministry, the presbyteral and the diaconal . . . Ordination is by prayer and the laying on of hands and takes place within the context of Holy Communion . . . In common with other churches in the ordination of presbyters and deacons, the Methodist Church intends to ordain, not to a denomination, but to the presbyterate and the diaconate in the One Holy Catholic and Apostolic Church. It looks for the day when, in communion with the whole Church, such ministries are recognized and exercised in common.[37]

---

36 *Constitutional Practice and Discipline of the Methodist Church* (Methodist Conference, 2010), Standing Order 600.
37 *Methodist Worship Book* (London: Methodist Conference, 1999), [*MWB*] pp. 297–8.

4.4.16 The duties of a presbyter are set out in the examination of candidates for presbyteral ordination:

to preach by word and deed the Gospel of God's grace;
to declare God's forgiveness of sins to all who are penitent;
to baptize, to confirm and to preside at the celebration of the sacrament of Christ's body and blood;
to lead God's people in worship, prayer and service;
to minister Christ's love and compassion;
to serve others, in whom you serve the Lord himself.[38]

4.4.17 'In the Methodist Church, diaconal ministry is an office in its own right rather than a step toward the office of presbyter.'[39] For this reason, diaconal and presbyteral ordination is not sequential. 'Deacons are ordained to a ministry of service and pastoral care and seek to equip God's people for service in the world.'[40] The duties of a deacon are set out in the examination of candidates for diaconal ordination:

to assist God's people in worship and prayer;
to hold before them the needs and concerns of the world;
to minister Christ's love and compassion;
to visit and support the sick and the suffering;
to seek out the lost and the lonely;
and to help those you serve to offer their lives to God.[41]

4.4.18 The Methodist Church teaches that 'All Christians are called through their Baptism and by the hearing of God's word to ministry and service among the whole people of God and in the life of the world.'[42] Thus lay people serve in authorized forms of ministry, as local preachers, evangelists, pastoral visitors and class leaders. Presbyters and deacons have 'no exclusive title to the preaching

---

38 MWB, p. 302
39 *MWB*, p. 297.
40 *MWB*, p. 297.
41 *MWB*, p. 317.
42 *MWB*, p. 297.

of the gospel or the care of souls. These ministries are shared with them by others to whom also the Spirit divides his gifts severally as he wills'.[43] Although presbyters normally preside at the Lord's Supper, if a local church would otherwise be deprived of receiving the sacrament because of a ministerial shortage, the Conference may authorize named lay people or deacons to preside at the Lord's Supper in a specified circuit for a limited period of time under the direction of the superintendent minister. That only the Conference may so authorize is intended to preserve the connexional nature of the Methodist Church as represented by the person who presides at the celebration of the Lord's Supper in the local church. Deprivation of the sacrament remains the sole ground upon which anyone other than a presbyter may be authorized by the Conference to preside at the Lord's Supper.

4.4.19   The Methodist Church, though numerically smaller than the Church of England, is well represented in cities, towns and villages throughout England. The Methodist Church also has local churches in Wales and Scotland so is a church of three nations. In the twenty-first century the Methodist Church is intent on re-affirming its origins and founding *charisms* as a discipleship movement through a renewed emphasis on encouraging Christian discipleship. Today, the Methodist Church is a connexion or communion of local churches that: celebrate and proclaim the Gospel; contain a rich diversity of people united round the Lord's table; nourish their members with the means of grace; manifest commitment to justice and peace; serve the needs within their neighbourhood; and are characterized by hope and joy.[44]

4.5 The Church in Ecumenical Perspective

4.5.1   Ecumenical dialogue has led to convergence, though as yet not a sufficient consensus, among the historic churches in under-

---

43 *Deed of Union*, §4.
44 *CLP*, §5.5.

standing the nature of the Church. Building on previous ecumenical studies, including the landmark *Baptism, Eucharist and Ministry* (1982), the WCC Faith and Order Commission has recently produced a convergence statement entitled *The Nature and Mission of the Church: A Stage on the Way to a Common Statement* (2005). This convergence statement contains much that Anglicans and Methodists can affirm together concerning the Church.[45]

4.5.2   In particular, Anglicans and Methodists affirm the following summary statements made in *The Nature and Mission of the Church*:

The Church is called into being by the Father 'who so loved the world that he gave his only begotten Son, that whoever believes in him shall not perish, but have eternal life' (John 3.16) and who sent the Holy Spirit to lead these believers into all truth, reminding them of all that Jesus taught (cf. John 14.26). The Church is thus the creature of God's Word and of the Holy Spirit. It belongs to God, is God's gift and cannot exist by and for itself. Of its very nature it is missionary, called and sent to serve, as an instrument of the Word and the Spirit, as a witness to the Kingdom of God' (§9).

The Church is the communion of those who, by means of their encounter with the Word, stand in a living relationship with God, who speaks to them and calls forth their trustful response; it is the communion of the faithful (§10).

The Church is not merely the sum of individual believers in communion with God, nor primarily the mutual communion of individual believers among themselves. It is their common partaking

---

45 Cf. 'Response of the Methodist Church in Great Britain to The Nature and Mission of the Church (WCC Faith and Order Paper 198)', Methodist Conference Agenda (2009), pp. 108–22. 'A response to The Nature and Mission of the Church from The Faith and Order Advisory Group of the Church of England' London: Faith and Order Advisory Group, 2009.

in the life of God (2 Peter 1.4), who as Trinity is the source and focus of all communion. Thus the Church is both a divine and a human reality (§13).

The one, holy, catholic and apostolic Church is sign and instrument of God's intention and plan for the whole world. Already participating in the love and life of God, the Church is a prophetic sign which points beyond itself to the purpose of all creation, the fulfilment of the Kingdom of God (§43).

Diversity in unity and unity in diversity are gifts of God to the Church. Through the Holy Spirit God bestows diverse and complementary gifts on all the faithful for the common good, for service within the community and to the world (cf. 1 Corinthians 12.7 and 2 Corinthians 9.13). No one is self-sufficient. The disciples are called to be one, while enriched by their diversities – fully united, while respectful of the diversity of persons and community groups (cf. Acts 2, 15; Ephesians 2.15–16) (§60).

The communion of the Church is expressed in the communion between local churches, in each of which the fullness of the Church resides. The communion of the Church embraces local churches in each place and all places at all times. Local churches are held in the communion of the Church by the one Gospel, the one baptism and the one Lord's Supper, served by a common ministry. This communion of local churches is thus not an optional extra, but is an essential aspect of what it means to be the Church (§65).

The communion of local churches is sustained by the living elements of apostolicity and catholicity: Scripture, baptism, communion and the service of a common ministry. As 'bonds of communion' these gifts serve the authentic continuity of the life of the whole Church and help to sustain the local churches in a communion of truth and love. They are given to maintain the Church in integrity as the one Church of Jesus Christ, the same yesterday, today and tomorrow (§66).

110

4.5.3 The Ninth WCC Assembly held in Porto Alegre, Brazil, in 2006 adopted a text, *Called to be the One Church*, inviting member churches to continue their journey together as a further step towards full visible unity. This text contains a useful description of what it means to say that the Church is apostolic and catholic.

The Church as communion of believers is created by the Word of God, for it is through hearing the *proclamation of the gospel* that faith, by the action of His Holy Spirit, is awakened (Romans 10.17). Since the good news proclaimed to awaken faith is the good news handed down by the apostles, the Church created by it is *apostolic*. Built on the foundation of the apostles and prophets the Church is God's household, a *holy* temple in which the Holy Spirit lives and is active. By the power of the Holy Spirit believers grow into a holy temple in the Lord (Ephesians 2.21–22) (§4).

The *catholicity* of the Church expresses the fullness, integrity, and totality of its life in Christ through the Holy Spirit in all times and places. This mystery is expressed in each community of baptized believers in which the apostolic faith is confessed and lived, the gospel is proclaimed, and the sacraments are celebrated. Each church is the Church catholic and not simply a part of it. Each church is the Church catholic, but not the whole of it. Each church fulfils its catholicity when it is in communion with the other churches. We affirm that the catholicity of the Church is expressed most visibly in sharing holy communion and in a mutually recognized and reconciled ministry (§6).

The Church as the creation of God's Word and Spirit is a mystery, sign, and instrument of what God intends for the salvation of the world. The grace of God is expressed in the victory over sin given by Christ, and in the healing and wholeness of the human being. The kingdom of God can be perceived in a *reconciled and reconciling community* called to holiness: a community that strives to overcome the discriminations expressed in sinful social structures, and to work for the healing of divisions in its own life and for healing and unity in the human community. The Church participates in the reconciling ministry of Christ, who emptied himself, when it lives out its mission, affirming and renewing the image of God in all humanity and working alongside all those whose human dignity has been denied by economic, political, and social marginalisation (§10).

4.5.4   The nature of the Church is inseparable from its divine purpose. A theological understanding of the Church therefore incorporates a theological understanding of its divine purpose in God's world. *Called to be the One Church* contains a useful summary statement of the Church's divine purpose.

Mission is integral to the life of the Church. The Church in its mission expresses its calling to proclaim the Gospel and to offer the living Christ to the whole creation. The churches find themselves living alongside people of other living faiths and ideologies. As an instrument of God, who is sovereign over the whole creation, the Church is called to engage in dialogue and collaboration with them so that its *mission* brings about the good of all creatures and the well-being of the earth. All churches are called to struggle against sin in all its manifestations, within and around them, and to work with others to combat injustice, alleviate human suffering, overcome violence, and ensure fullness of life for all people (§11).

4.5.5   In the Anglican-Methodist Covenant (2003) the Methodist Church and the Church of England state a number of mutual affirmations concerning their ecclesial status. These mutual affirmations are made on the basis of a shared history, full agreement in the apostolic faith, shared theological understandings of the nature and mission of the Church and of its ministry and oversight, and agreement concerning the goal of full visible unity. Having stated what Anglicans and Methodist respectively teach about the nature of the Church, it is useful at this point to re-state these mutual

112

affirmations made by the Church of England and the Methodist Church:

1. We affirm one another's churches as true churches belonging to the One, Holy, Catholic and Apostolic Church of Jesus Christ and as truly participating in the apostolic mission of the whole people of God.
2. We affirm that in both our churches the word of God is authentically preached, and the sacraments of Baptism and the Eucharist are duly administered and celebrated.
3. We affirm that both our churches confess in word and life the apostolic faith revealed in the Holy Scriptures and set forth in the ecumenical Creeds.
4. We affirm that one another's ordained and lay ministries are given by God as instruments of God's grace, to build up the people of God in faith, hope and love, for the ministry of word, sacrament and pastoral care and to share in God's mission in the world.
5. We affirm that one another's ordained ministries possess both the inward call of the Holy Spirit and Christ's commission given through the Church.
6. We affirm that both our churches embody the conciliar, connexional nature of the Church and that communal, collegial and personal oversight (*episkope*) is exercised within them in various forms.
7. We affirm that there already exists a basis for agreement on the principles of episcopal oversight as a visible sign and instrument of the communion of the Church in time and space.

4.6 Recognising a Christian community as a church

4.6.1 From what the Church of England and the Methodist Church respectively teach about the Church itself, based on Scripture, it is possible to state a number of criteria by which it can be said that a particular Christian community is a church in the true sense of the term. For both the Church of England and the

Methodist Church the presence of all of the following elements is the necessary and sufficient condition for a particular Christian community to be recognized as a church:

1. A community of people who are called by God to be committed disciples of Jesus Christ and to live out their discipleship in the world;
2. A community that regularly assembles for Christian worship and is then sent out into the world to engage in mission and service;
3. A community in which the Gospel is proclaimed in ways that are appropriate to the lives of its members;
4. A community in which the Scriptures are regularly preached and taught;
5. A community in which baptism is conferred in appropriate circumstances as a rite of initiation into the Church;
6. A community that celebrates the Lord's Supper;
7. A community where pastoral responsibility and presidency at the Lord's Supper is exercised by the appropriate authorized ministry;
8. A community that is united to others through: mutual commitment; spiritual communion; structures of governance, oversight and communion; and an authorized ministry in common.

4.6.2 While there are other elements that could be considered desirable, together these eight constitute the defining set of ecclesial elements whose presence in a Christian community is sufficient for it to constitute a church so far as the Church of England and the Methodist Church are concerned. The presence of some, but not all, of these elements may indicate that a community is on the way to becoming a church, though it has not yet attained that state. That a Christian community does not contain all the necessary elements that enable it to be recognized as a church does not mean that it has no ecclesial status. Being the Church is not a case of all or nothing, but instead involves degrees.

5

Reason: Investigating Fresh Expressions in Relation to the Church

5.1 Responses to fresh expressions

5.1.1   In Chapter 1 it was noted that the *Fresh Expressions* initiative is an established feature of church life in numerous dioceses, deaneries, parishes, districts and circuits. In some case specially trained pioneer ministers support the development of diverse kinds of fresh expression. A wealth of publications promote the positive contribution that *Fresh Expressions* makes to the mission of the Church of England and the Methodist Church.

5.1.2   The vast majority of fresh expressions in the Church of England and the Methodist Church have been set up by parishes and circuits, motivated by a concern to engage more effectively with those in the community who are currently beyond the ambit of traditional churches. A relatively small number are initiatives of deaneries, dioceses, districts or some other sponsoring body. As was noted in Chapter 2, there are many stories emerging from fresh expressions which testify to their success in engaging with people who have had little previous contact with one of the historic churches or else have become disillusioned with, and detached from, traditional forms of church life.

5.1.3   However, some theological commentators argue that *Mission-Shaped* Church and the consequential development of fresh expressions do not constitute a satisfactory strategy for Christian mission.

In particular, the theological understanding of the Church which underpins fresh expressions has been criticized as being inadequate. This chapter investigates and attempts to assess the principal criticisms made against fresh expressions.

5.1.4   Briefly, the principal criticisms advanced by commentators are that fresh expressions:

* Promote a church-shaped mission rather than a mission-shaped Church;
* Stem from a limited view of the *Missio Dei*;
* Discourage active participation in the mission of the Church;
* Constitute a combined Evangelical-Liberal attack on territorial parishes;
* Neglect the role of the Church in salvation;
* Fail to give visible expression to the reconciling work of Christ;
* Amount to a rejection of Christian Tradition.

5.1.5   Drawing on the theological method outlined above in Chapter 1, the following sections consider each of these criticisms in turn, drawing on Scripture, the teaching of the Church of England and the Methodist Church, critical reason and Christian experience in order to assess their claims.

5.2 Fresh expressions promote a church-shaped mission rather than a mission-shaped Church

5.2.1   The criticism that fresh expressions promote a church-shaped mission rather than a mission-shaped Church has been powerfully voiced by John Hull.[1] Hull regards the distinction between

---

1 John M. Hull, *Mission-Shaped Church: A Theological Response* (London: SCM, 2006); John M. Hull, 'Mission-shaped and kingdom focused?', Steven Croft (ed.), *Mission-Shaped Questions: Defining issues for today's church* (London: Church House Publishing, 2008), pp. 114–132; John M. Hull, 'Only one way to walk with God', Louise Nelstrop and Martyn Percy (eds), *Evaluating Fresh Expressions: Explorations in Emerging Church* (Norwich: Canterbury Press, 2008), pp. 105–20.

these ideas as 'the difference between a mission that is essentially shaped by the interests and concerns of the Christian churches and a Church that, forgetful of itself, is ready to perceive and respond to the mission of God'.[2] A mission-shaped Church is one that fulfils its proper role as an agent and instrument of God's Kingdom. 'The church is a mission project, not the mission itself; the Kingdom of God is the object of the mission, and the life of Jesus continues to be manifest through the church as it witnesses to, embodies and proclaims the kingdom.'[3]

5.2.2   According to Hull, *Mission-Shaped Church* 'blurs and confuses' the distinction between the Church and the Kingdom of God. It simultaneously attributes too much and too little significance to the Church: too much because it identifies the growth of the Church (and specifically that of the Church of England) with the growth of the Kingdom; too little because it under values the Church's role as agent of the Kingdom in bringing about peace and justice. In treating numerical growth, rather than God's Kingdom, as the objective of Christian mission, *Mission-Shaped Church* manifests a distorted understanding of the Church.

5.2.3   As an agent of God's mission to 'restore the brokenness of humanity and to renew the face of the earth', the Church should be prophetic and less concerned to promote its well-being. Hull claims to 'respect the intentions of those who divide people in Britain into the churched and the un-churched, and see it as their mission to transfer as many people as possible from the latter category to the former'.[4] However, he does not believe that this distinction is fundamental to God's mission. A more basic distinction would be that between rich and poor, between those at home and the foreigner, between those who seek after power and those who set out to serve

2 Hull, 'Mission-shaped and kingdom focused?', p. 114.
3 Hull, *Mission-Shaped Church: A Theological Response*, p. 5.
4 Hull, *Mission-Shaped Church: A Theological Response*, p. 128.

their neighbours, between those who in the name of national interest are ready to renew nuclear weapons and those who seek for peace and equality among the nations. Properly understood, the mission of the Church is to address these distinctions, working prophetically to bring about the great reversals of which Jesus spoke in his earthly ministry. Hull asks: 'How can it be that the mission of God who wills that all people should be saved has been turned into a competitive ideology and an institution with the same survival instincts as any other institution?'[5]

5.2.4   The Bible, claims Hull, conceives the human relationship with God as 'essentially a horizontal relationship'. That is to say, 'God is loved through the neighbour, and obedience to God is shown through seeking after justice for others.'[6] Thus the language of salvation must be accompanied by faithful actions that express love of one's neighbour. A church cannot talk about justice and peace without immediately acting on its words. At the same time, a church cannot work for justice and peace without relating these to the coming of God's Kingdom through Jesus Christ.[7] This way of 'walking with God' is the criterion for assessing Christian communities that claim to be new forms of the Church.[8]

5.2.5   Despite his criticisms, Hull shares the desire of *Mission-Shaped Church* for the Church of England to be renewed through the development of new forms of the Church – provided that these are prophetic signs of the Kingdom of God. Hulls wants the Church of England to be 'a church that not only hears but does the word of God, a church that calls men and women, boys and girls into discipleship of Jesus'.[9]

---

5 Hull, *Mission-Shaped Church: A Theological Response*, p. 128.
6 Hull, 'Only one way to walk with God', p. 108.
7 Hull, 'Only one way to walk with God', pp. 118–120.
8 Hull, 'Only one way to walk with God', p. 120.
9 Hull, *Mission-Shaped Church: A Theological Response*, p. 36.

Assessment

5.2.6 Christians have a duty to engage in mission in its broadest sense and not in a way that is narrowly 'church-shaped'. The Scriptures affirm that the mission of the Church is part of God's plan to renew humankind along with the whole of creation.[10] The Church is called to be an agent of God's mission to 'restore the brokenness of humanity and renew the face of the earth'. Faith in God therefore involves love for neighbour and the pursuit of justice.

5.2.7 Hull rightly warns against conceiving the mission of the Church narrowly in terms of seeking converts without working for justice or caring for creation. As was noted above (§2.5.3), both Mission-Shaped Church and Fresh Expressions specifically affirm the 'Five marks of Mission'. The missiological intentions of fresh expressions should therefore clearly reflect the holistic vision expressed in the 'Five Marks of Mission'. Training for fresh expressions practitioners may need to give greater attention to the fact that making Christian disciples and working for justice belong together.[11] Still, a fresh expression that emphasizes the importance of making disciples is being entirely faithful to the core purpose of Christian mission.

5.2.8 Certain aspects of Hull's criticism of fresh expressions are inconsistent with the Church as portrayed in Scripture. In particular,

---

10 See, for example, Christopher J. H. Wright, *The Mission of God: Unlocking the bible's grand narrative* (Leicester: IVP, 2006). The key biblical texts are: Isaiah 58.1–7; Micah 6.8; James 2.1–17; and 1 John 3.16–18.

11 The 2001 *Micah Declaration* on integral mission similarly declares: 'It is not simply that evangelism and social involvement are to be done alongside each other. Rather, in integral mission our proclamation has social consequences as we call people to love and repentance in all areas of life. And our social involvement has evangelistic consequences as we bear witness to the transforming grace of Jesus Christ. If we ignore the world we betray the word of God which sends us out to serve the world. If we ignore the word of God we have nothing to bring to the world. Justice and justification by faith, worship and political action, the spiritual and the material, personal change and structural change belong together. As in the life of Jesus, being, doing and saying are at the heart of our integral task.'

Hull's perception that the human relationship with God is primarily 'horizontal' does not do justice to God's relationship with people as described in the Bible, where the patriarchs, prophets, psalmists and disciples are all portrayed as experiencing a direct relationship with God. Nor, apparently, does Hull attach much significance to the Great Commission (Matthew 28.18–20) to make disciples of all the nations. The followers of Jesus experience a personal relationship with him through baptism into his body; they are not merely people who relate to their neighbours in a certain way. Of course, it is true to say that the love of God necessarily involves love of neighbour. That is why the two great commandments – to love God and to love one's neighbour – contain in summary form the whole of the Law in the Old Testament. However, it is not the case, as Hull seems to suggest, that Christians enter into a relationship with God only by means of loving their neighbour. According to the New Testament, individuals enter into a relationship with God by hearing the Gospel, repenting of their sins, expressing faith in Christ, being baptised/receiving the Holy Spirit, and by living a life of Christian discipleship (see above, §3.4.5; cf. Romans 5.1–6.14).

5.2.9   Hull suggests that the distinction to which the Church should give most attention is not that between churched and un-churched, but between rich and poor, between native-born and foreigner, between those who act ethically and those who do not. Certainly, in the Scriptures these latter distinctions matter to God, who is concerned for the poor and foreigners, and that people should act ethically. But, in the Bible, God is also concerned that the un-churched should become the churched, not in a simplistic sense that people should start attending church services, but that they should become baptised disciples of Jesus Christ and thus participants in the paschal mystery of his death and resurrection, reconciled to God and to one another. This means, as *Mission-Shaped Church* affirms, but as Hull seems to deny, that a concern for numerical growth is a legitimate part of the Church's mission. The intention of fresh expressions to make disciples of Jesus and to see the Church grow is consistent with Scripture, though it is fair comment to point out that numerical growth is not the sole criterion of successful Christian mission.

5.2.10   Hull is critical of the suggestion in *Mission-Shaped Church* that the poor and marginalized might 'form their own communities of faith' in which to work together for change and renewal. Hull regards such a move as compelling the poor to remain in poverty, and the marginalized to form their own churches on the periphery. However, this is not the intention of *Mission-Shaped Church*. Experience suggests that poor and marginalized people struggle to find an identity and a voice in churches because of the dominance of the educated rich. *Mission-Shaped Church* suggests that it would be appropriate to encourage them to establish their own communities so that they can develop the resources to challenge their situation, as was the intention behind the development of Base Ecclesial Communities in South America. As in all situations where power is involved, however, it is debatable whether strategies intended to empower specific groups will actually achieve the intended outcome.

5.2.11   Hull correctly draws attention to the fact that *Mission-Shaped Church* does not address the ecumenical implications of fresh expressions. Admittedly, *Mission-Shaped Church* is an internal Anglican report, and Fresh Expressions is an avowedly ecumenical organisation. Still, the question remains as to whether and how fresh expressions can embrace the ecumenical agenda in the interest of Christian unity. In particular, how might the development of fresh expressions best express and serve the interests of the Anglican-Methodist Covenant?

5.2.12   Hull also correctly draws attention to the fact that *Mission-Shaped Church* does not address the interreligious implications of fresh expressions. Interfaith relations are a sensitive issue in multifaith, multicultural Britain in the twenty-first century. Further theological reflection is needed to reconcile the overtly evangelistic purpose of fresh expressions with the commitment of the Church of England and the Methodist Church to maintaining good relations with members of non-Christian religions. Both churches have produced resources that provide a useful starting point for theological reflection concerning mission and evangelism in relation to people of non-Christian religions.[12]

5.3 Fresh expressions stem from a limited view of the *Missio Dei*

5.3.1   Fresh expressions have been criticized as reflecting a limited understanding of the *Missio Dei* or God's mission in the world, a criticism similar to John Hull's assertion that they reflect a narrowly church-shaped mission. Roger Walton maintains that *Mission-Shaped* Church and much of the resulting literature envisages a one-way dynamic between the Church and the world. In this dynamic: 'The Church is the agent and the world the recipient. Rather than the Church moving to join the missionary God who is at work in many and various ways outside, the Church is the normative, if not the sole, agent of God's mission.'[13] This encourages 'a view of the Church in its missionary endeavours as always being the carrier of Christ, bringing him to the world and rarely, if ever, being a recipient from God anywhere other than the gathered church and from any sources other than the ecclesial community'.[14]

5.3.2   According to Walton, this understanding of mission claims too much for the Church in the world: 'the church . . .

---

12 A recent Church of England report on the subject, *Sharing the Gospel of Salvation* (GS Misc 956), is available online at: http://www.cofeanglican.org/about/gensynod/agendas/July2010/gsmisc/gsmisc956.pdf. A Methodist Church document *May I call you friend? Sharing Faith with People of Other Faith* (Methodist Conference, 2006) is also available online at: http://www.methodist.org.uk/index.cfm?fuseaction=churchlife.content&cmid=1680.
13 Roger Walton, 'Have we got the Missio Dei right?' *Epworth Review*, Vol. 35/3 (2008), pp. 39–51(p. 42).
14 Walton, 'Have we got the Missio Dei right?', p. 43.

has no monopoly on God's reign, may not claim it for itself, may not present itself as the realized kingdom of God over and against the world.'[15] A narrowly church-centred perception of the *Missio Dei* means that Christians fail to catch glimpses of God at work in the world. It also leads to a condescending attitude towards those among whom the Church ministers. Behind this approach is a form of Gnostic dualism that, by denigrating everything outside the Church, fails 'to seek the traces of God in creation, receive the scattering of divine gifts and behold God's immanent presence'.[16]

5.3.3 Contrary to what he sees as the one-way missionary dynamic of fresh expressions, Walton asserts that Christ is already present in the world in many different situations. Wherever forgiveness occurs; wherever the truth is told; wherever the abuse of power is challenged; wherever creativity blossoms; wherever people renounce their reliance on wealth: 'these are the places where Christ may be said to be present and may be encountered.'[17] Christ is also present in 'communities of practice', which form people and enable them to flourish. Examples of such communities are found in work, education, friends and family. The Church is one of these communities: 'not so much as *the* Body of Christ but as a Body of Christ, allowing for other ways of Christ to be known in the world'.[18] The role of the Church, as manifested in the local church, is to be a 'facilitating agency', allowing people to discern the presence of Christ at work in the world.

5.3.4 For Walton, then, the world is not the place into which Christians foray to win converts for Christ, but the place where individuals may be formed by Christ into the persons they are called

---

15 Walton, 'Have we got the Missio Dei right?', p. 43. Walton quotes David Bosch.
16 Walton, 'Have we got the Missio Dei right?', pp. 44–6.
17 Walton, 'Have we got the Missio Dei right?', p. 47. Walton draws on Clive Marsh, *Christ in Practice: A Christology of Everyday Life* (London: DLT, 2006).
18 Walton, 'Have we got the Missio Dei right?', p. 48.

to be, and where they can bear witness to God's transformative power. By attending to the Christian story, the Church helps individuals to discover grace and develop the confidence to take risks. The Church is the place where experiences are gathered and interpreted so that Christians may be better equipped to worship and engage with God's world. Mission in this perspective means truly noticing what God is doing and joining in.[19]

Assessment

5.3.5   Walton, like Hull, offers a corrective against a possible tendency to view Christian mission as narrowly church-shaped. Anglicans and Methodists affirm that God is at work beyond the visible boundaries of the Church. The Anglican-Methodist Covenant declares that the Church's mission addresses people 'in all their social, economic, political and cultural relationships':

> Within that reality of human living and dying, loving and striving, suffering and rejoicing, God is already at work. We do not attempt to bring an absent Christ to an abandoned world. Mission is grounded on the theological conviction that Christ is already present to the world through the continual operation of the Holy Spirit. The mission of God to the world is constant and is not restricted to the Church (cf. John 3.16, 5.17). God is at work in communities, organisations and institutions that may have little or no overt connection with the Church except through the Christian believers who serve and witness within them. God may also use these bodies for the advancement of the Kingdom. They may even have something to teach the Church about what the Kingdom means, even though they may not explicitly acknowledge God's reign of justice and peace. The Church's witness is to the Christ who is at work in his universal mission and is known in his revealed gospel.[20]

---

19 Walton, 'Have we got the Missio Dei right?', p. 49.
20 *An Anglican-Methodist Covenant*, p. 30.

5.3.6   The Scriptures likewise affirm Christ's presence in the world in different ways, such as in the poor (Matthew 25). However, to suggest that the Church is not *the* body of Christ, but a body of Christ alongside others, lacks any foundation in Scripture. The only entity described in the New Testament as the body of Christ is the Church itself.[21]

5.3.7   Although Christ is present in the world in many different situations, Anglicans and Methodists affirm that the *mode* of Christ's presence in the Church is qualitatively different to his presence in the world. Christ is encountered in a distinctive way in the Church: in the proclamation of the Gospel; in the celebration of the sacraments; in the gathering of Christians for worship and fellowship. The presence of Christ in the world can only be recognized as such because his presence is first recognized in the Church.[22] In that specific sense the missionary dynamic can indeed be said to be one-way – from the Church to the world.

5.3.8   Walton implies that there is no real difference in the relationship between Christ and believers on the one hand, and between Christ and non-believers on the other. Yet, the Scriptures describe a fundamental difference in these two relationships. Only the Church can be the body of Christ because it is only in the Church that people are united to Christ through faith and baptism. In the New Testament the difference between believers and non-believers is not epistemological: that is to say, it is not primarily a matter of knowledge so that those inside the Church know more about the presence of Christ in the world than those outside. Rather, the difference is ontological: it relates to the very being of

---

21 Romans 12.3–8; 1 Corinthians 12.12–31; Ephesians 4.4–16; Colossians 1.18.

22 In Acts 17.22–31 and Romans 1.18–32 God makes himself known to all human beings through his creation and providence. Yet human beings do not benefit from this revelation. Rather they remain in ignorance, putting their trust in things other than God, and behaving in ways that merit God's wrath. It is only those in the Church who are saved from this situation.

individuals. Those who belong to the Church are those who have been united to Christ in baptism and are therefore a new creation (2 Corinthians 5.17).[23]

5.3.9   The role of the Church in the *Missio Dei* is more significant than that of a 'facilitating agency', enabling individuals to recognize Christ's presence in the world. Christian mission is concerned to incorporate people into the paschal mystery of the death and resurrection of Christ through faith and baptism. The *Missio Dei* is necessarily church-shaped because the Church is the visible body of Christ in the world, sign and foretaste as well as instrument of God's Kingdom. Insofar as fresh expressions are concerned to proclaim the Gospel and incorporate people into the body of Christ they can be said to fulfil the mission of the Church. Thus it is vital that fresh expressions practitioners are fully aware of the need for fresh expressions to be orientated to the Church.

5.4 Fresh expressions discourage active participation in the mission of the Church

5.4.1   It has been claimed that fresh expressions discourage active participation in the mission of the Church. Martyn Percy locates the Fresh Expressions initiative in the context of two contrasting models of religious belonging in Britain and Europe. In the 'market model', membership of the Church is essentially voluntary and associational, so that individuals choose to become members of the Church. In the 'utility model', Church membership is ascribed

---

23 The question of who ultimately belongs to the Church is beyond the scope of this present report. There are no limits to the grace and mercy of God. For a discussion of this issue from a Church of England perspective see the Doctrine Commission report *The Mystery of Salvation* (London: CHP, 1995), Chapter 7. For the Methodist position see *Methodist Doctrine and the Preaching of Universalism* (1992); reprinted in *Statements and Reports of the Methodist Church on Faith and Order*, Vol. 2 1984–2000 (Methodist Conference, 2000), pp. 580–91.

rather than chosen, so that individuals belong unless they opt out.[24] Percy refers to these types of belonging as 'intensive' and 'extensive', with corresponding implications for ministry. An 'intensive' ministry is primarily concerned with the spiritual well-being of individuals; an 'extensive' ministry is primarily concerned with service to those in the wider community.

5.4.2   In Percy's estimation there is an unresolved tension or ambiguity in fresh expressions between intensive and extensive types of membership and ministry. This leaves the Fresh Expressions initiative confused as to its aims and what is, and is not, properly described as 'church'.

> The diversity of projects, encounters and ideas seems to be almost limitless, suggesting that the identity of the movement is very much caught up in the sense of this being centred on evangelism for a post-institutional generation. (And perhaps post-ecclesial; but not post-spiritual or post-Christian?) This must partly account for why the official fresh expressions web site is rather coy about ecclesiology. It acknowledges that definitions of the Church are 'difficult', and that fresh expressions are therefore not easy to define.[25]

5.4.3   Underneath this 'playful ambivalence about what may or may not be church', Percy discerns potential problems, including a tendency for fresh expressions to gather round a single interest, issue or cause that is attractive and promises a clear return on a focused investment. This tendency undervalues the extensive ministry of the Church of England in unremarkable places and situations. Yet it is the Church of England's extensive ministry that is responsible for sustaining the nation's social and spiritual capital.[26] By focusing on intensive ministry in a small group, fresh expressions

---

24 Martyn Percy, 'Old tricks for new dogs? A critique of fresh expressions', Louise Nelstrop and Martyn Percy (eds), *Evaluating Fresh Expressions: Explorations in Emerging Church* (Norwich: Canterbury Press, 2008), pp. 27–39 (p. 30).
25 Percy, 'Old tricks for new dogs?', p. 36.
26 Percy, 'Old tricks for new dogs?', p. 37.

thus undermine the capacity of the Church of England to fulfil its extensive ministry. In Percy's estimation: 'it would seem that many individual fresh expressions are made up of those who are weary of the church as an institution, but still desire fellowship and individual spiritual sustenance. Seen from this perspective, the fresh expressions movement, despite its claims to the contrary, is a form of collusion with the endemic post-institutionalism in contemporary culture.'[27]

5.4.4 Furthermore, according to Percy, some fresh expressions practitioners positively embrace a post-institutional ethos, arguing that a fresh expression is 'church for people who no longer join bodies or associations'. This whole approach undermines the claims of Christian discipleship: 'Belonging together in a body with higher purposes places demands on individuals and groups, including those of duty and service; this is discipleship. Demand-led groups, in contrast, may just service people's desire for more meaning and fulfilment, while vesting this in the language of purpose, connection and even sacrifice.'[28]

5.4.5 Despite his strong criticisms, Percy believes that 'fresh expressions can make a modest and positive contribution to the mixed economy of church life'. He contends that the task facing the Church of England is to allow the 'effervescence' of movements such as fresh expressions to 'challenge and feed' it, while maintaining the parochial forms of mission that go on each day and are often unsung. Even so, the Church of England should not imagine that spiritual forms of post-institutionalism hold out any long-term hope for its future.

What is now deemed to be fresh cannot last, by definition. The task of the church, sometimes, is just to wait, and hope, pray and work for better times. It is after all one of the major themes

---

27 Percy, 'Old tricks for new dogs?', p. 31.
28 Percy, 'Old tricks for new dogs?', p. 31.

of the Old Testament: waiting. We know that the period of exile may indeed be very long. But the answer is not to be found in turning our gaze to the new gods of a very different kind of Babylonian captivity.[29]

Assessment

5.4.6   The nature of religious belonging is much debated at the present time.[30] The distinction between market and utility models of Church membership, between intensive and extensive ministry, can usefully be applied in seeking to describe the full shape of the Church's mission. An Anglican parish church offers an extensive ministry to everyone who lives in the parish, irrespective of whether they opt in to membership of the Church. Such a ministry can readily be affirmed as helping to sustain the social and spiritual capital of the nation. Percy's critique provides a necessary corrective to a possible tendency to undervalue the extensive ministry of the Church of England just because it is not perceived to be as attractive or apparently as successful as some other forms of mission.

5.4.7   Nevertheless, extensive and intensive membership and ministry are not mutually exclusive, as Percy seems to imply, but belong together within the mission of the Church. Alongside its extensive ministry to the parish, the Church of England also exercises an intensive ministry in the sense of building up the Christian life of the worshipping community within the parish. For without such a community at the heart of every parish it would not be possible to sustain an extensive ministry to others. The rite of confirmation denotes, in effect, a form of intensive membership.

5.4.8   That extensive and intensive types of membership and ministry are not easily untangled is also evident in the case of the

---

29   Percy, 'Old tricks for new dogs?', p. 39.
30   For an introduction see Grace Davie, *Religion in Britain since 1945: Believing without Belonging* (Oxford: Wiley Blackwell, 1994).

Methodist Church. Although the Methodist Church does not have a parish system as such, local churches relate to a particular neighbourhood. Applying Percy's categories, membership in the Methodist Church is intensive because it is voluntary and not based on a territorial parish. Contrary to Percy, however, this does not in fact result in a sharp disjunction between those who are in and those who are out of membership since the ministry of the Methodist Church is available to everyone living in a neighbourhood, even if that neighbourhood cannot be neatly defined in terms of parish boundaries. Given the widespread lack of knowledge of doctrinal differences among Christians, people do not necessarily discriminate when seeking the ministry and support of the Church. Thus the extensive ministry of the Methodist Church, like that of the Church of England (and other churches), helps sustain the social and spiritual capital of the nation.

5.4.9   The idea of extensive membership whereby people belong to the Church unless they intentionally opt out may make sense within a Christendom concept of a national Church in a Christian land; but it is hardly credible in a secular society where many people profess to have no religious beliefs. To the extent that fresh expressions involve intensive membership and ministry, this reflects contemporary Christian experience that the Church of England and the Methodist Church are engaged in mission in a largely non-Christian context.

5.4.10   Although the extensive ministry of the Church of England may be *available* to everyone in the parish, for various reasons not all the potential recipients wish to avail themselves of it. Historically, the mission of the Methodist Church has been among those people that the Anglican parish church, for whatever reason, has been least effective in reaching. Nowadays the Methodist Church finds itself in a similar position to the Church of England in that many of its local churches are increasingly ineffective in reaching a large section of the community. Accordingly, the Fresh Expressions initiative seeks to develop both an extensive and intensive ministry within that section of the population that is effectively beyond the ambit of Anglican parish churches and local Methodist churches.[31]

5.4.11 Doubtless, there will continue to be debate within the Church of England and the Methodist concerning appropriate strategies for mission and whether these should be broadly based or else narrowly focused on particular groups or sections of the population. The history of the global expansion of the Church contains examples of both approaches. Ideally, a church will reflect the diversity of the population living in its immediate surroundings, though a territorial perspective does not necessarily ensure that an Anglican parish church or a local Methodist church contains the full range of people living in that parish or neighbourhood. By raising concerns about inclusion and exclusion in relation to fresh expressions, Percy points to a wider issue facing Christian mission which requires more detailed study.

5.4.12 On the whole, Percy's assertion that fresh expressions collude with secular trends, knowingly or otherwise, to produce a post-institutional spirituality is not borne out by the evidence. Certainly, the Fresh Expressions initiative does not intend to encourage the establishment of Christian communities that are either independent or semi-detached from the sponsoring church, though some fresh expressions practitioners might be susceptible to thinking that way. The real issue here concerns how to ensure that fresh expressions remain accountable to the appropriate authority in the sponsoring church and how they may be encouraged to develop and strengthen relations.

5.4.13 Percy's assertion that fresh expressions discourage people from accepting the demands of Christian discipleship in favour of receiving congenial spiritual sustenance is no more possible to

---

31 For example, *Sorted and Re:generation* referred to in chapter 2 above are serious attempts to provide ministry to young people in the particular areas which they cover in a way that complements the work of the existing churches in those neighbourhoods. Those running them are not doing so for their own benefit, but for the benefit of the young people involved.

prove or disprove than the suggestion that traditional churches typically do the same thing. The mission of the Church is to press the claims of Christian discipleship with its radical implications for personal and corporate life.

5.4.14 To avoid becoming an excessive drain on scarce financial resources, fresh expressions could reasonably be expected to make a realistic contribution towards the cost of maintaining the ministry they receive from the sponsoring church and also to contribute to the cost of ministerial training. The interdependence and connectivity of all Christians within the body of Christ implies the need for such mutual support. This reflects the Church in the Acts of the Apostles where this kind of relationship existed between the mother church in Jerusalem and the new churches of the Gentile mission. These churches became self-supporting and also provided resources to support the churches in Judaea and Jerusalem in time of famine as an expression of their interdependence within the body of Christ (see above, §3.8.2).

5.4.15 It is reasonable to ask for patience as the Church of England and the Methodist Church reflect upon the most appropriate strategy for mission in the twenty-first century. However, the call for patience can sometimes be a pretext for maintaining the status quo. There is an appropriate form of impatience, which provides the impetus for change in institutions that might otherwise be resistant to change. Of course, the proper motivation for developing a fresh expression (or any other kind of mission project) is not simply impatience with existing forms of the Church but rather the desire to take advantage of a distinct opportunity for mission that otherwise could not be undertaken as effectively in any other way. Spiritual discernment is needed in order to establish when patience is appropriate and when it is appropriate to find new ways of responding to opportunities for mission.

5.4.16 Providing adequate resources to develop fresh expressions amid competing demands presents a challenge for Anglicans and

Methodists, especially in the present global economic crisis. The allocation of scarce resources of finance and personnel requires spiritual discernment as to what a mission strategy may realistically be expected to achieve, though churches have not always been good at establishing criteria of success and failure against which to measure missionary activities. This may well have to change in future. Even though it is neither possible nor desirable to subject Christian mission to the kind of cost-benefit analysis routinely found in the business world, ecclesiastical finances cannot be overlooked when resources are finite.

5.5 Fresh expressions constitute a combined Evangelical-Liberal attack on territorial parishes

5.5.1 Fresh expressions have been criticized for constituting an attack on the parish system (and ultimately an attack on the establishment of the Church of England) by undermining parish-based mission. John Milbank contends that the Fresh Expressions initiative stems from a tacit alliance in the Church of England between Conservative Evangelicals and Liberals, neither of which have much interest in the establishment of the Church of England, its parish system, or prescribed forms of worship. Conservative Evangelicals look upon all these as inimical to mission, and 'post-1960s theological liberals' regard all physical and social manifestations of the Church as 'unnecessary encumberances to the true work of self-knowledge and self-realization'. [32]

5.5.2 The supposed collusion between Conservative Evangelicals and Liberals is 'a clear conspiracy against the parish'. Milbank is trenchant in his criticism of the result:

---

32 John Milbank, 'Stale Expressions: The Management-Shaped Church', *Studies in Christian Ethics*, 21/1 (2008), pp. 117–28 (p. 123–4). See also, Graham James, 'Mission and the Parish-Shaped Church', *Theology* CIX/847 (2006), pp. 3–11.

Perfectly viable parishes, especially in the countryside or the semi-countryside, are increasingly deprived of clergy who are seconded to dubious administrative tasks or else to various modes of 'alternative ministry' such as 'ministry to sports people' or 'ministry to youth.' In all this there lies no new expression of church, but rather its blasphemous denial. The Church *cannot* be found amongst the merely like-minded, who associate together to share in a particular taste, hobby or perversion. It can only be found where many different peoples possessing many different gifts collaborate in order to produce a divine human community in one specific location. St. Paul wrote to Galatia and Corinth, not to regiments or weaving-clubs for widows. He insisted on a unity that emerges from the harmonious blending of differences. Hence the idea that the church should 'plant' itself in various sordid and airless interstices of our contemporary world, instead of calling people 'to come to church', is wrongheaded, because the refusal to come out of oneself and *go* to church is simply the refusal of church *per se*. One can't set up a church in a Café amongst a gang of youths who like skateboarding because all this does is promote skateboarding and dysfunctional escapist maleness, along with the type of private but extra-ecclesial security offered by the notion of 'being saved'.[33]

5.5.3 According to Milbank, the universal Church is located 'in one place, within one circumscribed boundary and in one sacred, consecrated building'. This building, in a specific place, images the cosmos, the human person and the transition of human history to the *eschaton*. 'Only in such a building can Christian worship be fully realized. And only in such a building can human beings come together simply as human beings, rather than as political, economic or religious beings.'[34]

5.5.4 A parish system that enables the residents in a particular place to come together for worship is 'simply the logic of ecclesiology

---

33 Milbank, 'Stale Expressions', p. 124.
34 Milbank, 'Stale Expressions', p. 125.

itself'. The only way for the Church to include everyone is to exercise a territorial ministry. 'Only pure geography encompasses all without exception. Equally, only the located place, situated round the buried bones of the martyrs, or even upon the site of obscure pagan anticipations of the coming of Christ, extends this embrace back into the mists of historical time and forward into a trusted future.'[35]

5.5.5 Milbank rejects the claim made by proponents of fresh expressions that 'people's orientation to the places where they live is in decline' (cf. above, §2.1.12). For Milbank, such claims are exaggerated 'because the desire of people to identify with where they live is so innate and so strong'.[36] Nor should the Church of England condone or endorse a decline in the significance of 'place' in people's lives; for not every trend in human relationships and communications is compatible with the Gospel.[37] Networking, associations and shared interest groups cannot substitute for real, embodied human relationships in a particular place. The Church is required to struggle against those things that detract from such relationships, not to accept them as a neutral development. The Anglican parish church stands as a bulwark against the erosion of the significance of place in human life. Moreover, by being at the centre of a local community, the parish church promotes a physical ecology based on sustainable local production.[38]

Assessment

5.5.6 Milbank's warning against the uncritical endorsement of a network society has to be taken seriously. The literature most often cited in support of Fresh Expressions tends to promote methods of mission in a network society without considering whether

---

35 Milbank, 'Stale Expressions', p. 125.
36 Milbank, 'Stale Expressions', p. 126.
37 Milbank, 'Stale Expressions', p. 127.
38 Milbank, 'Stale Expressions', p. 128.

this social trend should be challenged. If the 'incarnational principle' is truly at the heart of Fresh Expressions, then 'place' is more significant for human life than is suggested by the development of fresh expressions based on social networks. The physical presence of Anglican parish churches and local Methodist churches in a neighbourhood affirms the significance of 'place' in human life.[39] Spiritual communities based on particular places strengthen the wider community.

5.5.7   On the whole, Milbank's claim that fresh expressions constitute an attack on the parish system is not borne out by the evidence. The Fresh Expressions initiative accepts the need for a mixed economy in which fresh expressions complement, but do not replace, traditional churches.[40] The vast majority of fresh expressions in the Church of England are parish initiatives (§2.1.14; §5.1.2); a relatively small number are extra-parochial. A positive desire to reach the non-churched through fresh expressions does not constitute an attack on the parish system. It is conceivable that parish churches could be weakened as a result of investing energy and resources in a fresh expression, but it is equally possible that they will be enriched and encouraged.

5.5.8   Milbank appears to assert that the universal Church is to be found exclusively in (Anglican) parish churches – and preferably those ancient churches 'situated round the bones of the martyrs, or even upon the obscure pagan anticipations of the body of Christ'. Such a limited perception reduces the presence of the universal Church to an incredibly small compass. If Milbank is correct, then the implications for Christian mission would be immense. In

---

39 Parish names themselves ground the Church of England in a particular place. Similarly, the widespread Methodist practice of naming local churches after the town, village, neighbourhood, or even the street in which they stand, also grounds the Methodist Church in particular places.

40 Steven Croft, 'Formation for ministry in a mixed economy church', Louise Nelstrop and Martyn Percy (eds) *Evaluating Fresh Expressions: Explorations in Emerging Church* (Norwich: Canterbury Press, 2008), pp. 40–6.

particular, it would mean that: the Church cannot be found in any places of worship that do not belong to the Church of England; it is not present in any non-parochial places of worship (such as hospital or school chapels); it cannot be found in a daughter church of an Anglican parish; and that it is not fully present in the vast majority of Anglican parish churches that are not situated round the bones of the martyrs or on ancient pagan sites.

5.5.9 Limiting the presence of the universal Church to specific buildings – however venerable their foundation on the bones of the martyrs – has no basis in Scripture. The Church in the Acts of the Apostles was not tied to specific buildings but met wherever was most convenient for its mission. The development of dedicated church buildings is something that only seems to have happened in the course of the third century. The churches in Galatia and Corinth to which Milbank refers were not parish churches but collections of house churches meeting in private homes and drawing on networks of extended households or the many trade associations that were a feature of Greco-Roman society in the first century.[41] None of the elements of the universal Church as described in the New Testament requires the use of dedicated buildings.

5.5.10 Neither the Church of England nor the Methodist Church accept that the presence of the universal Church is restricted to specific buildings. On the contrary, the Church is present wherever the Gospel is rightly preached and the sacraments duly administered. So far as discerning the concrete location of the Church is concerned, buildings are not among the criteria for assessing whether the Gospel is rightly preached or the sacraments duly administered. The Church has met in all kinds of different architectural settings in the course of its history.

---

41 See Wayne A. Meeks, *The First Urban Christians: The social world of the Apostle Paul*, 2nd edn, (New Haven and London: Yale University Press, 2003), pp. 75–7.

5.5.11   Nevertheless, Anglicans and Methodists have a large number of buildings in use as places of worship. These have become sacred places as a result of their consecration or dedication for Christian worship and through their continual use for that purpose over a considerable number of years. Church buildings are a valuable missionary resource, a permanent visible witness to the Gospel in the surrounding area. A theology of sacred space/place encourages the architectural setting of Christian worship to reflect Anglican and Methodist beliefs concerning the nature of the Church itself. Many Christians cherish the sacred symbolism of their place of worship and find such symbolism conducive to worship. But fresh expressions that meet outside sacred buildings may do so partly because it is felt that architectural religious symbolism is so far removed from the everyday experience of the non-churched that it is a barrier to evangelism. On the other hand, a fresh expression meeting in a sacred building may be able to exploit the latent appreciation of Christian symbolism in a culture that is open to exploring the spiritual dimension of material things. Indeed, as Milbank clearly appreciates, the power of Christian symbolism should not be underestimated.

5.6 Fresh expressions neglect the role of the Church in salvation

5.6.1   It has been claimed that fresh expressions neglect the mediating role of the Church as the sacrament of salvation. Andrew Davison and Alison Milbank assert that *Mission-Shaped Church* and subsequently Fresh Expressions theorists, lacking a theology of *mediation*, describe the Church exclusively as the agent or instrument of God's Kingdom.[42] As such the visible Church is purely a human institution that exists only to serve the (often narrowly defined) purpose of God's mission in the world, a disposable instrument should it no longer be considered fit for purpose. For Davison and Milbank, the Church is not merely the agent of God's saving activity: it *is* God's saving activity. The structures of the Church are

42 Andrew Davison and Alison Milbank, *For the Parish: A Critique of Fresh Expressions* (London: SCM, 2010), chapter 3.

salvific and therefore not disposable. As the sacrament of salvation, the Church is the goal, as well as the means, of mission.

5.6.2   According to Davison and Milbank, fresh expressions theorists tend to distinguish between the Church and its mission. Such a distinction is false because the Church is central to what is proclaimed in Christian mission. The Church cannot be written out of the Gospel, because the Church is part of the faith professed in the historic creeds. Nor can the Church be sidelined by using Kingdom language instead.[43] Christian salvation is ecclesial in character.

Assessment

5.6.3   The Church of England and the Methodist Church each affirm that the Church is sign, instrument and foretaste of the Kingdom of God (cf. §4.5.2). Davison and Milbank rightly warn of the danger of neglecting these dimensions of the Church. *Mission-Shaped* Church affirms that the Church is an *instrument*, but says little about the Church as *sign*, and virtually nothing about the Church as *foretaste* of God's Kingdom. To be fair, *Mission-Shaped Church* was not intended to provide a theological account of the Church. In affirming that the Church is God's instrument, *Mission-Shaped Church* does not thereby deny that it is also a sign and foretaste of the Kingdom. The real issue is to what extent fresh expressions actually fulfil the vocation of the Church to be sign and foretaste, as well as instrument, of God's Kingdom.

5.6.4   In this regard it is significant that the Fresh Expressions initiative affirms the significance of the Church for the Christian life. Whereas some evangelistic enterprises might regard incorporation into the visible Church as less important for converts to Christianity, the whole purpose of fresh expressions is specifically to establish new forms of the Church.

---

43 Davison and Milbank, *For the Parish*, p. 60.

5.6.5   The mission strategy underlying the Fresh Expressions initiative is not necessarily incompatible with maintaining the kind of Catholic emphasis on the role of the Church in salvation which Davison and Milbank seek to preserve. For example, a number of fresh expressions within the Church of England seek to uphold the significance of the sacraments.[44] At the same time, reflecting the 'catholic and reformed' heritage of both churches, there is a legitimate diversity of theological emphasis among Anglicans and Methodists concerning the proper role of the Church in salvation. For some, the proclamation of the Gospel is itself powerful in mediating salvation in way that does not obviously rely on any mediation on the part of the Church. However, it is a false dichotomy to choose between the Word and the Church as being decisive in the mediation of salvation. The Church stems from the proclamation of the Gospel; the proclamation of the Gospel stems from the Church. It is therefore important that fresh expressions do not give the impression that the Church is merely the product of mission; for the Church itself, as the sacrament of salvation, is also a means of grace.

5.7 Fresh expressions fail to give visible expression to the reconciling work of Christ

5.7.1   Davison and Milbank argue that the Fresh Expressions initiative is misguided in encouraging the development of 'niche churches' that cater for particular networks of people with a shared culture or common interest. Niche churches do not give visible expression to the reconciling work of Christ. While fresh expressions theorists would accept that Christians must be reconciled to one another, they legitimize niche churches by postponing reconciliation until the *eschaton* or else by reducing it to an abstract, invisible idea lacking in meaningful content. Either way, niche churches have no need of visible reconciliation with other communities beyond a

---

44 See Steven Croft and Ian Mobsby (eds), *Fresh Expressions in the Sacramental Tradition* (Norwich: Canterbury Press, 2009).

voluntary affiliation for an agreed mutual benefit. Reconciliation is then either a reality that belongs to the distant future or else a present reality that makes no practical difference to Christian living.[45]

5.7.2   For Davison and Milbank, therein lies a failure to recognize that salvation is corporate and that reconciliation must be worked out in the particular. Christian redemption is more than the sum of individual reconciliations with God. Reconciliation with God entails reconciliation with fellow Christians. The corporate dimension of salvation is expressed in membership of a particular church that is in communion with other churches. The Church bears witness to a unity that is local as well as universal. If unity is understood to exist only at the universal level, then it remains an abstract idea and not a concrete reality.[46]

5.7.3   Davison and Milbank contend that the idea of establishing niche churches results from a mission strategy that consists in 'giving people what they want'. When churches compete with one another to give people what they want, there is little scope for voicing criticism of culture or issuing uncomfortable calls for social reform. A niche church is susceptible to turning a blind eye to the sins of its own constituency, while condemning the sins of other sections of society.[47] As a result, the Church loses her capacity for prophetic judgement.

5.7.4   In contrast, the Anglican parish church, say Davison and Milbank, is able to resist succumbing to sectional interests because it is a mixed community. Furthermore, it is precisely in this mixed community that the reconciling power of the Gospel is mediated and realized, represented and worked out in human relationships. The parish church bears witness in its neighbourhood to the comprehensiveness of the universal Church.[48]

---

45 Davison and Milbank, *For the Parish*, pp. 70–71.
46 Davison and Milbank, *For the Parish*, p. 72.
47 Davison and Milbank, *For the Parish*, p. 88.
48 Davison and Milbank, *For the Parish*, p. 92.

Assessment

5.7.5   The Church of England and the Methodist Church maintain that reconciliation with God has a corporate dimension and that the Church is the community of faithful people. Davison and Milbank rightly draw attention to the ecclesial dimension of salvation which is firmly attested in Scripture. St Paul affirms that the reconciliation between Jews and Gentiles achieved through Christ's death and resurrection needs to be expressed in the life of the churches. Writing to the mixed Jewish-Gentile church in Rome, he declares:

> May the God of steadfastness and encouragement grant you to live in such harmony with one another, in accord with Christ Jesus, that together you may with one voice glorify the God and Father of our Lord Jesus Christ. Welcome one another therefore, as Christ has welcomed you, for the glory of God (Romans 15.5–7).

5.7.6   Davison and Milbank rightly caution that 'giving people what they want' is not an appropriate mission strategy if this involves compromising the Gospel. The Pastoral Epistles warn that 'the time is coming when people will not put up with sound doctrine, but having itching ears, they will accumulate for themselves teachers to suit their own desires' (2 Timothy 4.3). This does not mean, however, that the Church should ignore the mission context. Accommodating the Gospel to particular cultures has always been a guiding principle in the global Christian mission.

5.7.7   While there is a danger that niche churches will reinforce sectional prejudices, it does not necessarily follow that Christian mission should avoid catering for particular sections of the population. The history of the Church provides striking examples of mission within the limitations imposed by culture. A feature of Christian mission in India, for instance, has been the establishment of churches for particular castes within Indian society. While perpetuating the Indian caste system in the Church would be contrary to the Gospel, caste-based churches can be regarded as a temporary expedient in the context of Indian society. The existence of black majority churches in Britain likewise reflects the importance of cultural heritage. Doubtless, debate will continue concerning the extent to which Christian mission should accept the constraints imposed by cultural norms and expectations. But the fact is that Christian mission has done so in the past and will almost certainly continue to do so in future. The significance of culture for the proclamation of the Gospel arises in connection with all forms of Christian mission and not solely in the case of fresh expressions.

5.7.8   Although a niche church would constitute an impaired sign of reconciliation, this need not mean that it has no value at all as such a sign. In theory, a territorial church bears witness to the universality of God's saving activity by being a mixed community; but in fact this is seldom the case. All too often, Anglican and Methodists congregations are predominantly white, middle class, female and elderly. This similarly impairs, but does not invalidate, their capacity to be a sign of God's reconciliation. All churches and Christian communities should strive to become more effective signs of reconciliation by being inclusive communities.

5.7.9   Expediency is a significant factor in the development of fresh expressions. The experience of fresh expressions practitioners is that the most effective way of reaching those sections of the population that are under-represented in traditional churches is by establishing new communities that present and embody the Gospel in culturally relevant ways.[49] The strength of this approach is that it enhances the catholicity of the Church by reaching people who are currently outside the Church. The weakness is that it leads to

---

49 It should perhaps be noted that this not a new idea. In the nineteenth century for instance both Anglicans and Methodists engaged in mission activity targeted at groups such as cab drivers, navvies, railway workers and seamen and the development of industrial mission in the twentieth century was part of the same tradition.

the development of Christian communities that are more likely to be unrepresentative of the general population.

5.7.10   All churches are called to become a better sign of reconciliation. This means that a fresh expression that was set up to cater for the needs of a particular culture or interest group must neither exclude others nor remain focused solely on that group. Moreover, a fresh expression should help its members to understand that they belong to the universal Church, which embraces many different kinds of people and cultures. Fresh expressions should therefore challenge prejudice and seek to promote personal and communal links with the wider Church.

5.7.11   Authorized ministers have an important role in this regard, linking individual churches and fresh expressions to the Church of England or the Methodist Church, and thereby to the universal Church. This is why it would be problematic for a fresh expression to seek to appoint its own ministers or to authorize one of its members to preside at the celebration of Holy Communion. Such a move would represent a rejection of catholicity and cause a serious breach with the universal Church.

5.8 Fresh expressions amount to a rejection of Christian Tradition

5.8.1   It has been claimed that fresh expressions amount to an outright rejection of Christian Tradition in favour of a radical re-invention of the Church. Davison and Milbank contend that fresh expressions prefer novelty to stability, valuing freedom of choice above the constraints of Anglican tradition. Symptomatically, fresh expressions manifest a selective approach to the Anglican liturgical tradition, preferring liturgical innovation to prescribed forms of worship.[50] In general, fresh expressions favour the universal and abstract, as against the particular and concrete. This is reflected in

---

50 Davison and Milbank, For the Parish, pp. 93–118. For an example of alternative approaches to worship see Jonny Baker, *Curating Worship* (London: SPCK, 2010).

the way that *Mission-Shaped Church* and Fresh Expressions theorists refer to 'church' and 'faith' rather than to 'the Church' and 'the faith'.[51]

5.8.2   For Davison and Milbank, a rejection of Anglican tradition indicates a reluctance to learn from the past.[52] As a result, fresh expressions in the Church of England lack a clear sense of Anglican identity.[53] Their liturgies and forms of life lack coherence and a foundation in Anglican tradition.[54] Fresh expressions fulfil the desire of the middle classes for novelty, while ignoring the need for stability and security which is important to the elderly, the poor and the perplexed.[55] They also create pastoral problems inasmuch as those whose faith has been nurtured in a fresh expression may be lost to the Church should they move to a different area and encounter unfamiliar forms of worship.[56]

5.8.3   According to Davison and Milbank, the rejection of Anglican tradition stems from an uncritical acceptance of the suppositions of post-modernity. It is an underlying post-modern perspective that encourages fresh expressions theorists to attach such little value to locality, history and the particular. Neglect of the liturgical life and discipline of the Church of England spiritualizes the Christian life in a way that undervalues human embodiment in a specific time and place.[57] A basic problem with the fresh expressions 'movement' is that it:

accepts and celebrates so many of the mistakes of post modernity, fragmentation, consumer culture, the primacy of choice, the slow triumph of the virtual and the eclipse of the local and the particular. It does this just as the world may be waking up to

51 Davison and Milbank, *For the Parish*, pp. 113–16.
52 Davison and Milbank, *For the Parish*, pp. 106–7.
53 Davison and Milbank, *For the Parish*, pp. 93–6.
54 Davison and Milbank, *For the Parish*, pp. 109–12.
55 Davison and Milbank, *For the Parish*, pp. 101–2.
56 Davison and Milbank, *For the Parish*, pp. 99–100.
57 Davison and Milbank, *For the Parish*, p. 117.

the need for something better, for the sake of our communities, for the sake of the planet and for the sake of our souls.[58]

5.8.4   Davison and Milbank envisage a role for fresh expressions within a re-invigorated parish system. Proper concern for 'Christian nurture and maturity' means that parishes and fresh expressions can work together to mutual advantage. Rather than being autonomous mission activities, fresh expressions should be developed exclusively as parish mission initiatives. The creative energy displayed by fresh expressions practitioners should encourage parishes to rediscover local possibilities for mission. In turn, the parishes provide an earthed community for the purposes of Christian education and practical discipleship.[59] Organizing fresh expressions as parish initiatives would benefit their leaders by making available theological resources and support.[60]

5.8.5   Davison and Milbank perceive a tension in the Church of England between its traditional emphasis on the liturgy 'as the principal place where Christians are taught and grow in discipleship' and its encouragement of fresh expressions to develop as 'forms of Church of England life almost entirely dispensed from liturgical expectations'.[61] They question whether it is wise to steer new converts, or those returning to the Church, away from parish churches, since growth in Christian maturity involves submission to the disciplines of the Church.

Assessment

5.8.6   The implications that post-modernity holds for Christian theology is disputed, and it is unlikely that a single study will resolve debate concerning the proper contribution of the past to the

---

58 Davison and Milbank, *For the Parish*, p. 118.
59 Davison and Milbank, *For the Parish*, p. 227.
60 Davison and Milbank, *For the Parish*, p. 227.
61 Davison and Milbank, *For the Parish*, p. 227.

contemporary understanding of the nature of the Church, or the most appropriate strategy for Christian mission in the twenty-first century. Davison and Milbank rightly draw attention to the dangers of privileging contemporary experience over Christian Tradition in theological reflection on the nature of the Church.

5.8.7   It is reasonable to suppose that many fresh expressions will be heavily influenced by practitioners whose attitude to Christian Tradition has been shaped by their own formative experience of the Church in a variety of ecclesial traditions that reflect varying degrees of appreciation for what has been received from the past. Not all fresh expressions practitioners are neglectful of the past, though it is probably true to say that the majority will at least have some reservations about aspects of Christian Tradition as this has been received in their particular ecclesial tradition; otherwise they would not devote so much time and energy to the development of fresh expressions. Given the complex way in which formative Christian experience is shaped by the received Tradition, consciously or otherwise, it would be simplistic to suppose that fresh expressions practitioners and their communities are dismissive of the past in a way that amounts to a deliberate rejection of Christian Tradition.

5.8.8   Nor would it be correct to assume that it is only fresh expressions that undervalue Christian Tradition and what has been inherited from the past. Anglican parish churches and local Methodist churches may similarly lack a genuine appreciation of Christian Tradition and a sense of their inherited Anglican or Methodist tradition and identity. Equally, they may prefer novelty to prescribed or authorized forms of worship, and generally sit lightly to their inherited tradition and identity. Insofar as there may be a lack of appreciation for Christian Tradition at the present time, the problem is not confined to fresh expressions.

5.8.9   In fact, it is not clear that fresh expressions are actually rejecting the past as much as offering a creative response to the challenges and opportunities presented by the contemporary missionary context. If fresh expressions sit lightly to the past, it is because they are intended to embody the dynamic nature of Christian Tradition. It has long been recognized that Christian Tradition is not a static deposit to be transmitted intact to successive generations but an inheritance that develops in response to changing circumstances.[62] John Henry Newman argued that, as in nature, change and adaptation in the life of the Church are not signs of decay, but rather of energy and vigour. As Newman famously put it: 'in a higher world it is otherwise, but here below to live is to change, and to be perfect is to have changed often'.[63]

5.8.10 The Church of England affirms the dynamic nature of Christian Tradition, as expressed in recent ecumenical dialogue with Roman Catholics: 'Tradition is a dynamic process, communicating to each generation what was delivered once for all to the apostolic community.'[64] Likewise, 'Methodists can welcome the recent ecumenical emphasis on tradition as dynamic, rather than static, as a shared, "lived experience", rather than simply a deposit of doctrine.'[65] In a dynamic Christian Tradition, receiving the wisdom of the past is not a passive act but a process involving active discernment.

Throughout the centuries, the Church receives and acknowledges as a gracious gift from God all that it recognizes as a true expression of the Tradition which has been once for all delivered to the apostles. This reception is at one and the same time an act of faithfulness and of freedom. The Church must continue faithful so that the Christ who comes in glory will recognize in the Church the community he founded; it must be free to receive the

---

62 See Owen Chadwick, *From Bossuet to Newman*, 2nd edn (Cambridge: Cambridge University Press, 1987).
63 John Henry Newman, *Essay on the Development of Doctrine* 6th edn (Notre Dame, Indiana: University of Notre Dame, 1989), 1:7.
64 ARCIC, *The Gift of Authority* (London, Toronto and New York: Catholic Truth Society/Anglican Book Centre/Church House Publishing, 1998), p. 11.
65 *CLP*, §3.1.17.

apostolic tradition in new ways according to the situations by which it is confronted.[66]

5.8.11   The performance analogy set out in Chapter 1 above illustrates the way in which Christian Tradition should be employed in the Church. There the life of the Church was described in terms of performing the drama of God's action in the world as recorded in the Scriptures. Such a performance involves improvisation as the Church encounters new situations in its progress through history. Improvisation requires attentiveness to Scripture, to the classic performance of Scripture within Christian Tradition, and to current Christian experience. The contemporary performance of Scripture does not consist merely in replicating the classical performance of the past.

5.8.12   As far as fresh expressions are concerned, fidelity to the Anglican and Methodist traditions does not require the undiscerning adoption of received liturgical practices and patterns of ecclesial life, irrespective of whether these are thought to be appropriate in a particular missionary context. Inculturation of the Gospel also involves the inculturation of Christian Tradition. While *Mission-Shaped Church* emphasizes the importance of inculturation (see above §2.5.4), it underestimates the problems involved in a cross-cultural process of this kind. The frequently employed image of 'planting the seed' of the Gospel in a different cultural soil assumes that it is possible to distinguish between the original seed and the various kinds of cultural soil in which the Gospel has been planted down the centuries. The extent to which it is even possible to distinguish in all respects between the form and content of the Gospel is debatable. The process of inculturation therefore requires spiritual discernment based on a sound knowledge of Christian Tradition and the reasons why it has been transmitted down the centuries. Such knowledge is not always evident among those who would set aside the received Anglican or Methodist traditions on the grounds that it has little value in the contemporary missionary context.

---

66 *The Gift of Authority*, p. 15.

5.8.13 It is important that fresh expressions practitioners possess a sound knowledge of the Anglican or Methodist tradition as appropriate. Part of their nurturing role in a fresh expression is to help new Christians understand and appreciate Christian Tradition so that they can come to play a full part in shaping and transmitting it to future generations.

5.8.14 Davison and Milbank argue that all fresh expressions in the Church of England should be parish mission initiatives. Certainly, Anglican parish churches have a vital role to play in initiating mission, as do local Methodist churches.[67] However, not all will have the resources to develop fresh expressions. Moreover, the intended membership of a fresh expression may cross the boundaries of several Anglican parishes or fall within the neighbourhood of more than one local Methodist church. Given the imperative for Christians to engage in mission, in these circumstances it would seem preferable for fresh expressions to be developed as deanery or circuit initiatives (or by some other body) than for nothing at all to happen. On the whole, it seems unnecessarily restrictive to insist upon all fresh expressions being mission initiatives of Anglican parish churches or local Methodist churches.

5.8.15 Davison and Milbank criticize the way in which *Mission-Shaped Church* and Fresh Expressions theorists tend to refer to 'church' and 'faith' in an abstract way (see above, §5.8.1). Some fresh expressions theorists would not regard this as a cause for concern. To their way of thinking, the question of whether a fresh expression is 'a church' within '*the* Church' is beside the point. What really matters is that a fresh expression is 'church' because 'church' is not to be thought of primarily as something that can be identified by the presence of certain structures or elements but as something that happens. Church, they would say, is an event and not an institution.

---

67 See Paul Avis, *A Church Drawing Near* (London: T&T Clark, 2003).

5.8.16   All the same, it makes no sense theologically to refer to 'church' in an abstract and insubstantial way.[68] As was noted above in Chapter 3, the Church in the Acts of the Apostles is always concrete and particular, even when a universal reference is intended. The Scriptures never refer to 'church' as an abstract entity but instead always refer to '*the* Church'. There are many images in the New Testament to describe this entity: but they all denote a visible community. Christian Tradition likewise refers to 'the Church' as something concrete and particular. The legitimate use of 'event' language in relation to the Church should not be taken to imply that the Church has no visible form or historical continuity.

5.9 Conclusion

5.9.1   This chapter has investigated in turn each of the principal criticisms levied against fresh expressions. In so doing, the theological method set out above in Chapter 1 has been adopted. The method followed has been to apply critical reason to Scripture, Christian Tradition and contemporary Christian experience.

5.9.2   On the basis of the foregoing assessments it is now possible to conclude that the principal criticisms of fresh expressions do not provide convincing reasons to suppose that the mission strategy of the Church of England and the Methodist Church is seriously defective in its aim to develop a mixed economy of traditional churches and fresh expressions. Nevertheless, these criticisms raise important issues in relation to fresh expressions which cannot be dismissed. A number of practical safeguards are required in order to ensure that a mixed economy does not compromise the integrity of the Church. These safeguards are set out below in Chapter 7 in the form of recommendations made by the working party.

---

68 See, for example, Stephen Platten, 'Definitely not Church', *Theology* CX/853 (2007), pp. 3–9. Cf. Stephen Platten, 'The grammar of ministry and mission', *Theology* CXIII/875 (2010), pp. 348–56.

5.9.3   It is also evident that fresh expressions provide spiritual and theological insights into the nature of the Church which should be recognized and affirmed. The next chapter integrates these insights with Scripture and the teaching of the Church of England and the Methodist Church concerning the Church as a contribution to the development of a mission-shaped ecclesiology.

6

Towards a Mission-Shaped Ecclesiology

6.1 Ecclesial dynamics and fresh expressions

6.1.1   The particular contribution of fresh expressions towards the development of Anglican and Methodist ecclesiology lies in their living and breathing the *missionary dynamics* of the Church, rather than in any specific theological reflection on the essentials of the Church. As was noted above in Chapter 2, *Mission-Shaped Church* and Fresh Expressions literature avoid setting out precise theological definitions of key terms so as not to pre-judge what a fresh expression might eventually look like when it has developed into a mature form. The missionary dynamics of fresh expressions are orientated towards Jesus Christ (and thus also orientated towards his body, the Church) but are not pre-determined in such a way as to replicate traditional forms of the Church. From a fresh expressions perspective, all forms of the Church are provisional in nature and will continue to adapt in response to their changing context as new Christians enter the Church.

6.1.2   This does not mean, however, that the *ecclesial dynamics* of fresh expressions are either unknowable or wholly unpredictable in operation and effect. That Anglicans and Methodists confess their belief in one, holy, catholic and apostolic Church will influence the ecclesial dynamics of fresh expressions, though not in such a way that their mature form can be predicted with complete certainty. Properly understood, the creedal marks are signposts to guide the ecclesial journey of fresh expressions in the right direction – not destination markers to indicate the journey's end has been reached.

6.1.3   It is essential that from the outset the development of individual fresh expressions is informed by an awareness of the
creedal marks of the Church and by attentiveness to their cultiva-
tion. Fresh expressions should be consciously orientated towards
the one, holy, catholic and apostolic Church. This is necessary so
that the heart of what is given by God in the Church and how it is
given – in the ministry of word and sacrament – does not become
obscured, distorted or diluted as a fresh expression develops.

6.1.4   This chapter investigates the ecclesial dynamics of fresh
expressions in relation to the creedal marks of the Church with
the intention of discovering how they might inform good practice,
and how they might inform theological reflection on the Church. A
shared understanding of the ecclesial dynamics of fresh expressions
will contribute towards the development of a mission-shaped ecclesiology in which the Church is seen to be ordered and empowered
to fulfil God's mission in the world.

6.1.5   The principal ecclesial dynamics investigated in this chapter
are derived from the study of the Acts of the Apostles in Chapter 3
above, and are related to *intensivity* and *connectivity*. To recap,
intensivity consists in attentiveness to the teaching of the apostles,
the breaking of bread, and worship (§3.5.5). Connectivity consists
in apostolic oversight and support for the churches to ensure their
fidelity to the Scriptural tradition in witnessing to Jesus Christ
(§3.9.5). Integral to apostolic oversight is the authorization of local
ministry and frequent apostolic visitation so that Christian communities are accountable and the integrity of the Church is preserved (§3.5.6). By such means the mission of the Church remains
a connected activity in diverse places (§3.7.2).

6.1.6   The ecclesial dynamic of intensivity denotes the process
by which are forged the bonds of *koinonia* (fellowship, communion) that create and sustain a Christian community around the
apostolic teaching, the Eucharist and worship – that is to say,
around the ministry of word and sacrament. The ecclesial dynamic

of connectivity denotes the process by which are forged the bonds of *koinonia* that unite Christian communities within the universal Church. Though it is convenient to distinguish between these processes for the purpose of studying the Church, in reality they are so deeply related that they are the inseparable result of the work of the Holy Spirit. The authentic presence and effect of these ecclesial dynamics in Christian mission is to produce the unity, holiness, apostolicity and catholicity of the Church.

6.1.7   The ecclesial dynamics of fresh expressions, when properly orientated towards the one, holy, catholic and apostolic Church, will show signs of developing intensivity and connectivity. Needless to say, traditional churches should similarly be characterized by the ecclesial dynamics of intensivity and connectivity – not merely in an institutional sense but in the way these dynamics find expression in the Christian life, corporately and individually.

6.2 Intensivity as an ecclesial dynamic

6.2.1   One of the emphases of fresh expressions is a desire to strengthen Christian community and human community in response to the fragmentation of neighbourhood society. Typically, fresh expressions seek to provide a welcoming space for gathering and sharing together in activities that help form and build up community. Listening and responding to local needs therefore lies at the heart of the incarnational mission of fresh expressions. However, the essentials of Christian community are defined theologically and not sociologically. Christian community is not simply a heightened form of human community but is related in a particular way to Jesus Christ.

6.2.2   Christian community is based on *koinonia* with God through all the means of grace pledged to God's people. If a fresh expression is truly ecclesial in character then the ecclesial dynamic of intensivity will be reflected in its deliberate orientation to the ministry of word and sacrament. For the most intensive form of Christian community is found in the gathering round the proclamation of the Gospel and the celebration of the sacraments of baptism and the Lord's Supper. Since word and sacrament are God's unmerited gift to the Church, they are to be received with joy and gratitude which prevents the life of the Christian community from being reduced to one of anxious instrumental activity. The Church is foremost the community that receives (and then mediates) God's grace – it is not merely a missionary agency.

6.2.3   An orientation to the ministry of word and sacrament is not something that can be added subsequently to a fresh expression at some unspecified point in its development. Flour and eggs have to be added to the mix prior to baking a cake: they cannot be added at a later stage. Analogously, an orientation towards the ministry of word and sacrament is an essential ingredient in fresh expressions. Such an orientation will ensure that the dynamics at work in fresh expressions are truly ecclesial. Thus the ministry of word and sacrament, which binds the Church to God's gracious initiative, is foundational and integral to the development of fresh expressions.[1] A fresh expression may not yet be at a stage where the community is ready to celebrate the sacraments of baptism and the Eucharist, but preparation for that eventuality should be the intention and aim from the outset.

6.2.4   The ecclesial dynamic of intensivity has important implications for the training of ministers to work with fresh expressions. Such ministers are often referred to as 'pioneer' ministers to reflect their role in breaking new ground in mission. It is not enough for candidates to have energy, enthusiasm and a heart for Christian mission. They must be adequately trained and formed as pioneer ministers in relation to the ecclesial dynamics of intensivity and connectivity. Practical concerns about costs should not be allowed

---

1   Steven Croft, *Jesus' People: What the Church Should Do Next* (London: Church House Publishing, 2009), pp. 70ff.

to obscure the need for a satisfactory training strategy. Ministerial formation in the case of pioneer ministers requires sufficient resources, just as much as preparing ministers for parish and circuit ministry. Both kinds of ministry require the necessary skills and training to be able to form and build up Christian communities centred on the proclamation of the Gospel and the celebration of the sacraments in ways appropriate to their mission context. Both kinds of ministry will require sensitive pastoral, liturgical and reflective skills if they are faithfully to serve and lead their communities.

6.2.5   Fostering a love for the Scriptures requires biblical literacy; and an appreciation of the sacraments requires catechesis to understand their significance for the Christian life. Thus the Church of England and the Methodist Church need pioneer ministers who are themselves sufficiently formed in their knowledge and appreciation of the Scriptures and the sacraments as to be able to communicate their value to new Christian disciples. At the same time, the existence of fresh expressions should encourage Anglicans and Methodists to produce catechetical and liturgical resources that are readily applicable to mission contexts where there is little prior knowledge of Christianity.

6.2.6   A Christian community that is truly the Church, a visible sign of God's Kingdom, will manifest the reconciling power of the Gospel in fragmented human society; it will rise above diversity, self-interest and tribalism in order to point towards the full and final reconciliation of humankind in God. However, the Church on earth is an imperfect manifestation of reconciliation: 'The church reflects *in a broken fashion* the eschatological communion of the entire people of God with the triune God in God's new creation.'[2] Recognizing their frailty and imperfection, fresh expressions and traditional churches must continually strive to become better signs

---

2 Miroslav Volf, *After Our Likeness: The Church as the Image of the Trinity* (Grand Rapids, Michigan: Eerdmans, 1998), p. 235; emphasis added.

of God's Kingdom by expanding, diversifying and strengthening the Christian community.

6.2.7   The mutual reconciliation and commitment at the heart of Christian community is contrary to the egocentrism of post-modern culture. Likewise, the commitment to holy living is contrary to the pick-and-mix spirituality evident in postmodern culture. The Gospel is counter-cultural as well as cross-cultural. Yet it would be naive to suppose that the Church will remain impervious to the influence of post-modernity, including the consumerist culture in which personal choice is central. Throughout its history, the Church, whether consciously or otherwise, has been influenced by cultural changes, including the development of technology.

6.2.8   A consumerist culture need not be regarded as unpromising soil for Christian mission since an emphasis on personal choice is compatible with the Christian life. In the apostolic Church Christian discipleship was readily thought of as involving a day to day re-commitment, a daily act of self-denial (Luke 9.23). In a largely secular culture, a commitment to Christian discipleship similarly results from a conscious decision among a range of possible lifestyle choices. Jesus' parable warning against the accumulation of 'treasure on earth' (Matthew 6.19–21) speaks to a consumerist culture by offering a radical re-interpretation of utility and investment. It is worth noting that the Church in China is rapidly expanding in the context of a strongly consumerist culture.

6.2.9   The making of disciples cannot be separated from the formation of Christian community. The decision to become a Christian results in a set of relationships that demand mutual commitment, understanding and patience. None of this is foreign to *Mission-Shaped Church* and Fresh Expressions thinking, though the challenge is to find appropriate ways of orientating fresh expressions to the ministry of word and sacrament so that the ecclesial dynamic of intensity is preserved.

6.2.10   The ecclesial dynamic of intensivity, centred on word and sacrament, does not impede mission. On the contrary, in being constitutive of Christian community, word and sacrament are thereby also orientated towards mission. For gathering round the proclamation of the Gospel always involves a commissioning to be sent into the world to make new disciples of Jesus Christ. As Steven Croft explains: 'coming together to be with Jesus and being sent out in love and service to God's world. This, and only this, is what it means to be church: Jesus' people'.[3] Likewise, the celebration of the Lord's Supper empowers the community to engage in mission:

> . . . the Eucharist undergirds the mission of the Church. It unites Creation and Redemption, life and liturgy, porch and altar. It galvanizes Christians for witness and service in the world and strengthens us to go forth for Christ to win others to his cause. There is a real empowering in the Eucharist for all who are brought into communion with Christ and his people here. The Eucharist is central because mission is fundamental and mission cannot be separated from unity. The Eucharist is often called the sacrament of unity: it is equally the sacrament of mission.[4]

6.3 Connectivity as an ecclesial dynamic

6.3.1   Anglicans and Methodists affirm in their respective ways that connectivity belongs to the essence of the Church. For Anglicans, connectivity is expressed in deanery, diocesan and national synodical structures and in an authorized ministry of bishops, priests and deacons that is accepted throughout the Church of England. For Methodists, connectivity is similarly expressed in its connexional structures and an authorized ministry of presbyters

---

3 Croft, *Jesus' People*, pp. 52f.
4 *The Eucharist: Sacrament of Unity* (London: Church House Publishing, 2001), p. 5.

and deacons that is accepted throughout the Methodist Church. Those ordained as presbyters and deacons are accepted into 'Full Connexion' with the Conference to signify that their ministry embodies the connectedness of Methodism.

6.3.2   The *koinonia* between Christian communities is essentially the same as the *koinonia* within them: it is sacramental, spiritual and juridical. Spiritual *koinonia*, though real, is invisible. Sacramental and juridical *koinonia* gives visible and concrete content to the claim that Christians are reconciled to one another through the atoning sacrifice of Jesus Christ. Anglicans and Methodists consider that no individual Christian community can contain the fullness – the catholicity – of the Church without the ecclesial dynamic of connectivity being expressed in visible, concrete relationships with other Christian communities.[5]

6.3.3   Fresh expressions should not be a vehicle for autonomous missionary enterprises that are unconnected to the Church of England or the Methodist Church as appropriate. Thus the ecclesial dynamic of connectivity should be present in fresh expressions from the outset. If a fresh expression is truly ecclesial in character then the dynamic of connectivity will be expressed as an imperative towards maintaining visible links with other Christian communities through structures of communion.

6.3.4   Authorized ministers have an important role in expressing the connectivity of the Church. Ordained ministers in particular express the connectivity of the Church because they are bound together through their ordination into a common ministry. The intention of Anglicans and Methodists is to ordain into the ministry of the one, holy catholic and apostolic Church. As representative

---

5   'Life in self-sufficient isolation, which rejects the enrichment coming from other local churches as well as the sharing with them of gifts and resources, spiritual as well as material, is the denial of its very being.' ARCIC, *Church as Communion* (London: Church House Publishing, 1991), p. 26.

people, ordained ministers represent the universal Church to a particular Christian community and vice versa. In this way ordained ministers are a visible sign of the Church's connectivity, expressing in their person and ministry the *koinonia* that links a Christian community to the wider Church. Ministerial succession is a visible sign of the connectivity of the Church through time.

6.3.5   The ordained ministry is given by God not to exercise control but for building up the Church (cf. §3.7.2). The ordained ministry is therefore at the service of the baptised for the sake of the Church's mission and ministry in the world. This means that ordained ministry is never exercised autonomously but always under the appropriate ministry of oversight. In the Church of England it is bishops who properly exercise a ministry of oversight, assisted in various ways by archdeacons and other clergy. In the Methodist Church it is the Conference that properly exercises a ministry of oversight, assisted by Chairs of District and Circuit Superintendents. Fresh expressions and traditional churches are accountable to the relevant ministry of oversight.

6.3.6   Connectivity in fresh expressions is properly expressed through an authorized ministry that includes ordained and lay people as appropriate to the community's particular life and stage of development. Fresh expressions pioneers are not autonomous agents of mission but are subject to the ministry of oversight which they themselves represent in a particular setting. For Anglicans this means that pioneer ministers are accountable to the diocesan or area bishop and those who assist in the ministry of oversight, archdeacons, and rural and area deans. For Methodists this means that pioneer ministers are accountable to the Conference and those who assist in the ministry of oversight, usually the Circuit Superintendent. In this way pioneer ministers embody and uphold the ecclesial dynamic of connectivity in fresh expressions. Pioneer ministers have a key role in helping fresh expression relate to other Christian communities. While there is room for diversity, fresh expressions are not free to develop in ways that would

161

compromise connectivity by diverging from the common witness to Jesus Christ.

6.3.7 The ministry of oversight exercised by bishops in the Church of England and by the Methodist Conference has a special responsibility in guarding against diversity that threatens to impair connectivity. This responsibility is exercised in partnership with fresh expressions pioneers.

> The task of those entrusted with oversight, acting in the name of Christ, is to foster the promptings of the Spirit and to keep the community within the bounds of apostolic faith, to sustain and promote the Church's mission, by preaching, explaining and applying its truth. In responding to the insights of the community, and of the individual Christian, whose conscience is also moulded by the same Spirit, those exercising oversight seek to discern what is the mind of Christ. Discernment involves both heeding and sifting in order to assist the people of God in understanding, articulating and applying their faith.[6]

6.3.8 The reference to discernment as involving 'heeding and sifting' is echoed in what *Mission-Shaped Church* refers to as 'double-listening'. The ministry of oversight, assisted by fresh expressions pioneers and others, is charged with heeding and sifting the activities of mission and the Christian Tradition. Faithful imagination and creative responsibility are essential if this process of heeding and sifting is to bear authentic fruit and preserve the ecclesial dynamic of connectivity.

6.3.9 Spiritual discernment requires faithfulness to Scripture and Christian Tradition, as well as a willingness to listen to voices from the margins of the Church. The sensitive exercise of authority in the Church suggests the need for a 'safe space' where questions, plans, beliefs and practices can be tested candidly and without hasty

---

6   *Church as Communion*, p. 23.

judgement, and from where a 'new witness' to Christian Tradition can emerge.[7] This is consistent with the idea of a two-way channel of communication between the centre and the margins as described in the Acts of the Apostles (see above, §3.7.3; §3.9.5). Ultimately, the General Synod of the Church of England and the Methodist Conference may be called upon to exercise their respective discernment in a way that is comparable to the first Apostolic Council as recorded in the Acts of the Apostles (Acts 15; see above, §3.8).

6.3.10   It would be incorrect to regard the norms of Anglican or Methodist tradition as imposing unnecessarily restrictive rules that inhibit mission to contemporary people. The ecclesial dynamic of connectivity is intended to ensure that every Christian community at each stage of its development is gathered round what is recognizably the same ministry of word and sacrament. Thus the ecclesial dynamic of connectivity safeguards the ecclesial dynamic of intensity.

6.3.11   In order to embody connectivity and assist in the process of double-listening, fresh expressions practitioners require an appropriate knowledge of their respective ecclesial tradition and its purpose in the life of the Church. This strengthens the argument that pioneer ministers should be trained alongside those preparing for parish or circuit ministry.

6.3.12   Connectivity does not require uniformity (§6.3.7). There is a legitimate diversity in the development of fresh expressions in different contexts under the guidance of the Holy Spirit. However, the same Spirit is the Spirit of *koinonia* (2 Corinthians 13.13), who binds Christian communities into one communion or fellowship. Communion with God the Father through God

---

7   Laurie Green, *Let's Do Theology: A Pastoral Cycle Resource Book* (London and New York: Continuum, 1990), p. 93. The term 'safe space' comes from the Anglican Communion's Indaba Project. Here the role of bishops as convenors is to refine the questions for their own contexts, ensure diverse participation and to create a safe space for genuine conversation.

the Son in the power of God the Holy Spirit is what defines the Church and the object of its mission. To set aside practices and norms that create, nurture and sustain *koinonia*, on the ground that they apparently inhibit mission to the non-churched, would be to act in way that is contrary to the nature of the Church and its mission.

6.4 Resourcing a Mixed Economy Church

6.4.1   A mixed economy Church should not mean parallel spheres of ecclesial life and mission having little in common. Nor should it merely denote a loose alliance of communities affiliated by adherence to a common objective. In a mixed economy Church each part belongs to every other part in such a way that there is one body. United with others in the one body of Christ, Christian communities should not think of themselves as competitors in mission but instead be willing to work together, sharing resources and insights for the good of the whole.

6.4.2   A mixed economy Church requires a mission strategy in which what are, humanly speaking, scarce resources of finance and people are used to greatest effect at the service of God's mission in the world. This requires spiritual discernment and active collaboration among authorized ministers, who should be committed to listening to one another and praying together so that their common mission may bear fruit. It also requires an honest and realistic assessment of the opportunities and challenges posed by contemporary society.

6.4.3   The substantial cost of supporting fresh expressions in the Church of England and the Methodist Church raises practical questions: to what extent do fresh expressions represent a worthwhile investment of scarce resources? Can the investment of time, energy and finance be sustained over a long enough period of time for fresh expressions to bear fruit in terms of an increase in the number of

Christian disciples? What level of investment in fresh expressions would be proportionate to the expected return?[8]

6.4.4   These questions are difficult to answer. Some would argue that support for fresh expressions reflects the core values of the Gospel. Hence expecting a 'return' from an 'investment' in fresh expressions could be considered inappropriate. Yet the Church has also to consider the cost of ministerial stipends and employee salaries, pensions, housing, fuel, buildings maintenance and running costs. The actual cost of supporting fresh expressions and (in some cases) pioneer ministry therefore cannot be ignored.

6.4.5   In a mixed economy Church not all fresh expressions will prove to be sustainable over an extended period of time, even though they may undertake valuable work for a limited period. While fresh expressions are inherently risky enterprises, the reasons why some are not sustained require greater attention. Admittedly, objective criteria of success and failure are notoriously difficult to establish in Christian mission. All too often, bold claims of success are accepted at face value. The lessons of apparent failure are seldom learned in such a way that mistakes are not repeated. In exercising good stewardship of finite resources, the Church of England and the Methodist Church have a duty to reflect on the sustainability of fresh expressions in relation to their mission strategy.

6.4.6   In practice, the cost of supporting fresh expressions varies greatly according to type and the extent to which they are supported by pioneer ministers. In the case of fresh expressions meeting on church premises and led by parish or circuit ministers and lay volunteers, the cost is usually minimal. On the other hand,

---

8   When considering the cost of sustaining fresh expressions, it should be remembered that many Anglican parish churches and local Methodist churches are sustained to a certain extent by the proceeds from historic assets or from hiring out church premises rather than from the freewill financial giving of the congregation.

fresh expressions engaged in outreach among the poorest sections of the community and meeting away from church premises often require substantial financial investment from church funds since Government funding is usually only available on conditions that the churches find restrictive or unacceptable. Fresh expressions among the more affluent sections of the population might reasonably be expected to make an increasing financial contribution to their maintenance.[9]

6.4.7   For ecclesiological and pastoral reasons, fresh expressions should be developed with the necessary investment of authorized ministry, ordained and lay. It would be a mistake to suppose that simply recruiting a large number of untrained and unpaid lay pioneers would provide a solution to the problem of resourcing fresh expressions. This would be to neglect the ecclesial dynamic of intensivity, which requires an orientation to the ministry of word and sacrament from the beginning of a fresh expression. Moreover, it would place an unacceptable burden on individuals who lack the necessary training and ministerial formation to embody connectivity.

6.4.8   Nevertheless, there may be ways of reducing the cost of providing authorized ministry for fresh expressions. For example, the Church of England and the Methodist Church should consider whether and how suitable candidates for non-stipendiary ordained ministry might be identified among lay people working with fresh expressions. Non-stipendiary ordained ministers working in fresh expressions would have to receive the necessary training to embody the ecclesial dynamics of intensivity and connectivity. They should also be able to undertake the range of duties associated with ordained ministers because the ministry of the Church is at the service of all God's people.

---

9   This is happening in some cases. For example, *Contemplative Fire* is now financially independent of its sponsor, the Diocese of Oxford. http://www.contemplativefire. org/guide.htm#chap7.

6.5 Network and Neighbourhood Society

6.5.1 There is a difference of opinion among commentators about the implications for Christian mission and ecclesiology of the advent of a 'network society' that threatens to displace, to a certain extent, 'neighbourhood society' (cf. above, Chapter 5). Without entering into that debate, it is reasonable to suppose that Christian mission would at least want to engage with network society, if only to understand and evaluate its norms. While Christian mission should not be so accommodating towards contemporary culture as to lose sight of the counter-cultural implications of the Gospel, nor must it neglect the opportunity to embody Christian community in network society. The Church is therefore required simultaneously to be sensitive to cultural differences and critical of those aspects that would be corrosive of Christian community, identity and holy living.

6.5.2 Historically, Christian mission in Britain has proceeded on the assumption that the neighbourhood in which people live provides the primary context for relationships and the formation of community. However, there are signs (disputed by some) that contemporary society operates less through relationships formed within a physical environment and rather more on network relationships developed though employment, recreational pursuits and even electronic communications. This social trend is sometimes described as a transition from 'neighbourhood to network'. While such a description may be too simplistic, it is apparent that social networking is increasingly a feature of contemporary society with as yet unforeseeable consequences.

6.5.3 Insofar as it is a discernable trend, the transition from neighbourhood to network society generates a number of social problems to further complicate Christian mission. In particular, a self-selecting network society can easily become so withdrawn from the physical environment that the neighbourhood becomes neglected and dysfunctional. The main victims of this trend are the poor, the vulnerable and the elderly, who are less mobile and so less able to escape their physical neighbourhood to form social networks. In this situation, a legitimate aim of Christian mission is to reclaim or reconstitute human communities based on neighbourhood. The Anglican parish church and the local Methodist church have a crucial role in so doing because of their territorial mission and visible presence in a neighbourhood.

6.5.4   But the fragmentation of neighbourhood society is not due solely to the growth of social networks. In some cases neighbourhood society becomes fragmented because poverty, social deprivation, alcohol and substance abuse, and anti-social behaviour conspire to create a population that is divided, isolated and fearful, even in a relatively small and closely defined geographical area such as a particular housing estate. Often, the only community-building agencies left in these areas are local schools and churches. However, churches may well find the level of social problems to be far beyond their capacity or resources to address.

6.5.5   Idealistic descriptions of territorial mission tend to underestimate the difficulties involved in reclaiming or reconstituting human communities based on neighbourhood. Sociologically, the potential strength of a neighbourhood-based community will depend upon a combination of factors that are mostly beyond the capacity of the Church to influence. Thus neighbourhood society tends to flourish in those physical environments where family relationships are strong and the movement of population into and out of the area is low, and where there is economic equality. In many cases it helps if the physical environment is a well defined geographical area, and if the infrastructure and communications links are good. The presence of shared cultural values and identity also contributes to the strength of neighbourhood society.

6.5.6   For various reasons, all these factors have diminished in recent decades, leading to a widespread erosion of social capital. Even in a rural village – often perceived to be the ideal social setting for a Church of England parish – neighbourhood-based community is no longer a given fact. Here, as elsewhere, it is a struggle to create community among a population that is economically and emotionally detached from the physical environment, often because people are employed outside of the area. Widespread use of the word 'community' by local government authorities (as in community colleges, community schools, community leisure centres etc.) suggests a desire to strengthen what is perceived to be lacking in many places. Territorial-based Christian mission pursued through Anglican parish churches and local Methodist churches can both strengthen and benefit from neighbourhood community. However, given the erosion of neighbourhood community, it seems unlikely that territorial-based mission alone will be able to reach all sections of a deeply fragmented society.

6.5.7   It is in a deeply fragmented society that fresh expressions could make a significant contribution to Christian mission. Some of the most imaginative fresh expressions have been established in situations of great social deprivation. The Lighthouse Project in the Diocese of Winchester is one such example; its story is told below.

6.5.8   The transition from neighbourhood to network society, though a recognizable phenomenon, should not be overstated. As yet, few people inhabit a purely network society. In practice, communities are formed through a combination of neighbourhood and social networks. How the current balance will change in future depends on various factors such as the price of fuel, the state of the transport system and technological advances. There are also signs that the term 'local' has positive connotations in a society increasingly concerned about the adverse effects of globalisation and the erosion of community. Eventually, a pendulum effect may lead to a recovery of the value of neighbourhood as the primary context of community, though the precise impact of rapid technological developments, volatile social trends and uncertain economic conditions is difficult to predict.

6.5.9 Whatever theological reflection is required in the process, Christian mission does not usually wait for the dust to settle before responding to changing social conditions. Instead Christian mission engages with people in their immediate circumstances and cultural setting, even if it aims to transform these into something more appropriate for holy living. The social realities facing Christian mission in Britain at the present time were investigated at length in *Mission-Shaped Church*. Now Anglicans and Methodists might usefully develop a mission-shaped ecclesiology that overcomes the apparent dichotomy between neighbourhood society and network society by conceiving community as based on physical environment and social networks. The network-neighbourhood context of Christian mission and Christian community is here termed 'locality'.[10] Whereas territorial and network-based mission represent opposite poles, mission based on a locality consciously adopts a mediating position.

6.6 Intensivity and Connectivity in relation to Locality

6.6.1 Locality, then, is relational space based partly on neighbourhood and partly on social networks.[11] Locality occurs wherever human beings come together for some common purpose or shared activity. Traditional churches are natural centres of locality. Supermarkets, schools, pubs, clubs and other venues where people gather together are also centres of locality. Localities overlap with one another; they are fluid but not without recognizable structures and patterns.

6.6.2 A group of young people drawn together in the pursuit of a common interest or sport at a particular venue can be thought

---

10 This idea was adumbrated by Lesslie Newbigin, 'What is "a local church truly united"?', *Ecumenical Review* 29 (1977), pp. 115–28.

11 Due to geographical and cultural pluralism whereby humans inhabit more than one kind of environment, 'A purely territorial understanding of locality no longer seems meaningful today.' Volf, *After Our Likeness*, p. 277.

of as a constituting one such locality. A fresh expression based on that locality will embody a new kind of Christian community for neighbourhood-network society. At the same time, the ecclesial dynamics of intensivity and connectivity should lead to the development of a Christian community that transcends the limitations imposed by its locality. It is in transcending the limitations of its locality that a fresh expression grows towards maturity in the universal Church.

6.6.3   Christians are called to holy living in community with other Christians. The pursuit of holy living provides a perspective from which to assess the limitations imposed by locality, though the perspective of individuals and their community may need to be corrected by insights from external perspectives. That is true of all Christian communities and not just fresh expressions. It would be incorrect to suppose that traditional churches are necessarily better placed to judge how the limitations of their locality may have obscured aspects of the Gospel.

6.6.4   A mixed economy Church in the context of locality would combine territorial mission and network mission in an integrated and creative way. In fact, this is already happening as Anglican parish churches and local Methodist churches develop fresh expressions in localities beyond themselves. Territorial-based mission therefore has a secure future in a mixed economy Church.[12]

6.6.5   For convenience, the following table presents in summary form the respective emphases associated with the formation of Christian community in the three different mission contexts identified in this report – territorial, network, and locality. The table summarizes in broad terms the types of relationship, the means of development, and the style of governance in each.

---

12   As is affirmed by Robin Gamble, 'Doing traditional church really well', Steven Croft (ed.), *The Future of the Parish System: Shaping the Church of England for the Twenty-first Century* (London: CHP, 2006), pp. 93–109.

	Territorial	Locality	Network
Type of Relationships	neighbourly dutiful	Group-focussed	associational
Means of Expansion	Geographical Extension	Growth of group Relational	Individual Recruitment
Governance Style	Legislative	Self-Regulating	Unregulated

6.6.6   The idea of Christian mission in a locality as envisaged in this chapter is not a new phenomenon, though the type of social networks involved may be different. The history of overseas missions provides numerous examples of the evangelization of particular ethnic or social groups, whose cultural identity was subsequently incorporated into Christian communities.[13] The experience of overseas missions could usefully be applied to Christian mission in Britain.

6.7 Conclusion

6.7.1   A theological method that draws on Scripture, Tradition, reason and Christian experience is never content merely to repeat historical patterns uncritically, but will always seek to discern afresh the will of God for the Church. This chapter has investigated the ecclesial dynamics of intensivity and connectivity in relation to fresh expressions. A mission-shaped ecclesiology must take proper account of these ecclesial dynamics and the changing missionary context.

6.7.2   It should not be forgotten that the ecclesial dynamics of fresh expressions tend to involve people who are new to Christian faith and unfamiliar with many of the things that longstanding

---

13   For example, Vincent J. Donovan, *Christianity Rediscovered: An Epistle from the Masai* (Maryknoll: Orbis, 1982) tells the story of an African tribe's conversion to Christian faith.

Christians may take for granted. Unlike an Anglican parish church or local Methodist church, a fresh expression has no established Christian community into which new members can be absorbed. Usually there is little or no previous experience of Christian liturgy, the sacraments and the Scriptures. Embodying Christian community in these circumstances involves many challenges. Fresh expressions bring to the forefront the need for new and accessible forms of Christian worship, catechesis and spiritual formation suitable for contemporary mission contexts. A fresh expression reflects in an acute form the constant struggle of Christian communities to be both of their age and for their age.

6.7.3   There are many related ways of thinking of the Church. The Church is the body of Christ, the people of God gathered together under Christ's authority and vivified by the Holy Spirit, the first-fruits of a new creation (1 Corinthians 15.20ff). A fresh expression will truly be a fresh expression of *church* if it follows God's gracious initiative in two directions: the ecclesial dynamic of intensivity gathers a community round the ministry of word and sacrament; the ecclesial dynamic of connectivity leads the community into a visible relationship with other Christian communities.

6.7.4   A mixed economy Church will inevitably contain different perspectives, priorities and practices as past and present, old and new, encounter each other. The history of the Church reveals that maintaining unity in the face of the resulting tensions can be costly, but that disunity incurs an even greater cost as the Church's unity-in-mission is severely impaired.

The Lighthouse Project, Winchester Diocese

On the Weston Estate in Portsmouth people have chaotic lives, which make any form of commitment difficult. Though social structures are home-based, family life is fluid, with people constantly moving into and out of relationships. People expect to get what they want, when they want it. Their world is immediate and self-centred. They have low self-esteem. Many are in debt and have relational difficulties because of alcohol and substance abuse. Poverty also means that people's lives are confined to a neighbourhood in which they are obliged to live but which they do not love. Many rarely travel, even to nearby Southampton.

Insofar as people have any understanding of the Church, they do not think of themselves worthy of belonging to it. At the same time, they are suspicious that the Church is after their money. They find the local church building a threatening environment, a place to be avoided except possibly for occasional rites of passage.

The vision of the Anglican parish church, Holy Trinity, was that it needed to reach out into this non-churched community and establish a presence there. This objective has been achieved by the project leader living amongst the people he serves. Tim Hyde, a Church Army Captain lives in the heart of the estate. This is a profoundly incarnational mission, and a costly one for him and his family. Their struggle to live out their faith there gives honest testimony to Christ coming into the world.

This Christian presence is characterized in practical ways – by neighbourly love, home refurbishment and the provision of furniture, all offered freely (without expecting to receive anything in return) and as quickly as possible. Jesus is first proclaimed in deed, and then sometimes in word in the resulting conversations; but such proclamation is done sensitively and without pressure to respond. Serving the needs of the community demonstrates the recipient's worth and acceptance by the Church. Four projects run by the Lighthouse give the Church of England visibility on the estate, providing a way into people's lives by meeting them at their point of need.

The forms of service offered by these projects carry a *vocational* element. Just as Jesus began his ministry by calling together his disciples, the projects are not intended to keep people in a state of dependency but rather to form a community of mutual care and support. Through the forms of service offered, the projects create 'structures of participation'.[14] For example, the Lighthouse allotments, which people can dig as a remedy for depression, also provide free food for the estate, for the Sure Start agency and for the lunch club. Projects transcend tribal belonging, enhance the self-esteem of volunteers and serve the common good.

Tim uses the word 'church' of the work at Weston to reflect the intention of the project to create Christian community. Unlike social work, the project hopes for a communal response – in the first instance through gaining willing volunteers to share in the work. Initially, commitment to helping is usually weak and needs support so that the work can continue even if people don't show up. In a culture where people often shy away from responsibility, the Lighthouse is able to act as a prophetic sign of an alternative lifestyle. For this sign to be effective, however, there must be stability and a constant presence in the neighbourhood, which is expensive to maintain. Some public funding is available but is usually temporary and unpredictable. The Lighthouse project has been running for four years now but has barely begun to scratch the surface.

The long-term aim is to establish a worshipping community on the estate, based on a simple Gospel message: 'God loves us, God cares for us, God provides what is good for us and the work in which we are called to share.' A worshipping community on the estate would not make much use of liturgical texts. The celebration of the Eucharist is still a long way off, but this could be done through the link with Holy Trinity church. Currently, Tim shares in the cell structure of Holy Trinity church, which is not directly linked to the Lighthouse project.

Though some people on the estate know the benefits system well enough to enjoy a reasonable standard of living, many are in debt, often because of addiction to drugs and alcohol. Loan sharks are active on the estate. Clearly, the Church cannot

---

14 Ann Morisy, *Beyond the Good Samaritan: Community Ministry and Mission* (London: Mowbray, 1997), p. 25 *passim*.

expect to receive money from those living in such difficult circumstances, though it can hope for a return investment of time and energy from volunteers.

Lighthouse has been funded by the Church Army. The project started in November 2007 and its services are provided free at the point of delivery. The Church Army has designated the Lighthouse as a 'mission centre' suitable for the training of new officers, and a trainee officer has recently been appointed. The parish church has agreed to contribute financially to the costs of the Church Army, and Tim also receives funding from a number of individuals who support his work.

The valuable support of two diocesan officers on the project's management group is not represented in the immediate financial equation. Nor is the considerable investment in Tim's formation as an effective Church Army officer. It would be difficult to imagine the Lighthouse surviving without such trained leadership.

7

Conclusions and Recommendations

7.1 Summary Conclusions

7.1.1   The opening chapter of this report posed a number of practical and theological questions relating to fresh expressions before outlining the theological method adopted by the working party with particular reference to the doctrinal standards of the Church of England and the Methodist Church. The teaching of the Church of England and the Methodist Church concerning the nature of the Church is based on Scripture interpreted in the light of Christian Tradition, reason, and Christian experience. This teaching should not be thought of as a static deposit to be received and handed on intact. It is dynamic in the sense that its transmission from one generation to another involves its being re-shaped in response to changing circumstances. Adopting a performance analogy to reflect this dynamism, the particular task of the working party has been to discover what an authentic performance of the Scriptures will look like in the current missionary context in Britain in relation to the Church and fresh expressions.

7.1.2   Taking each element of this theological method in turn (experience, Scripture, Tradition and reason), the chapters following investigated: fresh expressions in Anglican and Methodist experience (Chapter 2); the Church in the Acts of the Apostles (Chapter 3); the Church in the Anglican and Methodist traditions (Chapter 4); and the principal theological criticisms made against fresh expressions. Recognizing how the transmission of Christian teaching is always responsive to the changing situation, the basic contours of a mission-shaped ecclesiology have been explored in relation to what the working party calls the ecclesial dynamics of intensivity and connectivity at work in fresh expressions (Chapter 6).

7.1.3   Drawing together the findings of these various investigations it is now possible to state briefly a number of summary conclusions that will be amplified in turn in the following sections of this final chapter of the working party's report:

- Fresh expressions, as part of a mixed economy Church, have a legitimate place in the mission strategy of the Church of England and the Methodist Church.
- The teaching of the Church of England and the Methodist Church concerning the nature of the Church itself provides the necessary theological and ecclesiastical framework for the development of fresh expressions.
- The principal theological criticisms that have been made against fresh expressions are not entirely justified but are nevertheless cautionary.
- From the outset fresh expressions should be orientated towards their eventual full expression of the Church's ministry of word and sacrament.
- From the outset fresh expressions should be orientated towards their eventual full expression of the *koinonia* (communion) of the Church.
- Fresh expressions are accountable to the relevant ministry of oversight in the Church of England and the Methodist Church and should be subject to normal ecclesiastical discipline.
- The development of fresh expressions requires authorized ministers with the necessary gifts and training.
- A mixed economy Church relies upon mutual trust, support and collaboration between traditional churches and fresh expressions.
- The wider implications of fresh expressions for the mission strategy of the Church of England and the Methodist Church require further investigation.

7.2 Fresh expressions, as part of a mixed economy Church, have a legitimate place in the mission strategy of the Church of England and the Methodist Church

7.2.1   The theological and missiological principles underpinning fresh expressions are consistent with the teaching of the Church of England and the Methodist Church concerning the nature of the Church and its mission.

7.2.2   There are no convincing reasons to doubt the proposal of *Mission-Shaped Church* that fresh forms of the Church are required for the sake of the Church's mission to a substantial proportion of the population whom traditional churches are currently not reaching.

7.2.3   The Church of England and the Methodist Church should affirm and support both the mission of parishes and circuits and the development of fresh expressions as part of a mixed economy Church.

7.3 The teaching of the Church of England and the Methodist Church concerning the nature of the Church itself provides the necessary theological and ecclesiastical framework for the development of fresh expressions

7.3.1   The intention and purpose of the doctrinal standards of the Church of England and the Methodist Church is to safeguard the integrity of the Church. They should therefore be upheld in their present form and applied consistently in all parts of the Church of England and the Methodist Church until such time as they are amended by an authoritative act of discernment.

7.3.2   For some, fresh expressions represent an unprecedented and radical innovation in Christian mission which requires Anglicans and Methodists urgently to revise their teaching about the nature of the Church. Others regard fresh expressions as part of a recurring phenomenon in the history of Christian mission which can and should be accommodated within the existing structures of the Church of England and the Methodist Church. The question will only be settled by an authoritative act of discernment. But whether the Church of England or the Methodist Church would consider itself to be in a position to decide one way or another in the next few years remains to be seen. The working party concludes that it would be premature at the present time to imagine that the doctrinal standards of the Church of England or the Methodist Church concerning the nature of the Church need to be substantially revised.

7.3.3   The question of whether fresh expressions are *new* forms of the Church (§1.3.1) is misleading in the light of Anglican and Methodist teaching on the Church. The doctrinal standards of the Church of England and the Methodist Church define a number of essential ecclesial elements that together constitute the Church. There can be no new form of the Church that does not contain all of these elements. In that sense new forms of the Church are all variations on this common set of ecclesial elements.

7.3.4   The term 'fresh expression of church' is potentially misleading. The Church is never an abstract theological concept because the body of Christ is always a visible, concrete reality in the world (§5.8.16). Anglicans and Methodists refer to '*the* Church', usually meaning the only, holy, catholic and apostolic Church; they also refer to '*a* church', usually meaning a particular Christian community that contains all the essential elements of *the* Church. The phrase 'fresh expression of church' should be interpreted in such a way that it clearly refers to *the* Church.

7.3.5   The teaching of the Church of England and the Methodist Church identifies eight essential ecclesial elements by which a particular Christian community can be identified as a church in the true sense of the term (§4.6.1). For emphasis these are repeated here. A church is:

1. A community of people who are called by God to be committed disciples of Jesus Christ and to live out their discipleship in the world;

2. A community that regularly assembles for Christian worship and is then sent out into the world to engage in mission and service;

3. A community in which the Gospel is proclaimed in ways that are appropriate to the lives of its members;

4. A community in which the Scriptures are regularly preached and taught;

5. A community in which baptism is conferred in appropriate circumstances as a rite of initiation into the Church;

6. A community that celebrates the Lord's Supper;

7. A community where pastoral responsibility and presidency at the Lord's Supper is exercised by the appropriate authorized ministry;

8. A community that is united to others through: mutual commitment; spiritual communion; structures of governance, oversight and communion; and an authorized ministry in common.

7.3.6   A Christian community that lacks some or all of these essential ecclesial elements is not a church, though this does not necessarily mean that it has no ecclesial status. It would be incorrect to describe such a community as 'a form of church for our changing culture' or as 'church for the people involved'. This would be to replace an objective definition with a subjective definition that sells short the Gospel and thus fails those whom it is intended to benefit.

7.4 The principal theological criticisms that have been made against fresh expressions are not entirely justified but are nevertheless cautionary

7.4.1   The principal theological criticisms made against fresh expressions were carefully examined in Chapter 5. The working party's conclusion is worth restating in full: 'the principal criticisms of fresh expressions do not provide convincing reasons to suppose that the mission strategy of the Church of England and the Methodist Church is seriously defective in its aim to develop a mixed economy of traditional churches and fresh expressions. Nevertheless, these criticisms raise important issues in relation to fresh expressions which cannot be dismissed. A number of practical safeguards are required in order to ensure that a mixed economy does not compromise the integrity of the Church' (§5.9.2). These practical safeguards are contained in the working party's recommendations below.

7.5 From the outset fresh expressions should be orientated towards their eventual full expression of the Church's ministry of word and sacrament

7.5.1   An authentic Christian community is characterized by the proclamation of the Gospel, worship and prayer, the celebration of baptism and the Lord's Supper, a commitment to discipleship and service, and mission in the world. From the outset fresh expressions should be orientated towards their eventual full expression of the Church's ministry of word and sacrament. To use the term employed elsewhere in this report, a fresh expression will manifest the ecclesial dynamic of intensivity (§6.2).

7.5.2   But whereas a traditional church absorbs new members into an existing community, the challenge and opportunity facing fresh expressions is that of embodying a new Christian community among people without much previous knowledge or experience of the Church. This requires the development of appropriate resources for worship and liturgy, catechesis in the faith, and spiritual guidance (§6.2.5).

7.5.3   As can be seen from the stories of individual fresh expressions that have been included in this report, as well as from numerous other stories that can be found on the Fresh Expressions website, this is a challenge which is being met with considerable imagination and energy. There are numerous examples of newly established Christian communities in the Church of England and the Methodist Church. These communities, which are at different stages of development, reflect the ecclesial dynamics of intensivity and connectivity on the way to becoming churches. They are finding creative ways to proclaim the Gospel afresh to people who have little or no previous contact with the Church.

7.6 From the outset fresh expressions should be orientated towards their eventual full expression of the *koinonia* (communion) of the Church

7.6.1 An authentic Christian community is one that is connected to other Christian communities by deep bonds of *koinonia* that include visible structures of communion, a ministry of oversight, and an authorized ministry in common. From the outset fresh expressions should be orientated towards their eventual full expression of the *koinonia* (communion) of the Church. To use the term employed elsewhere in this report, a fresh expression will manifest the ecclesial dynamic of connectivity (§6.3).

7.7 Fresh expressions are accountable to the relevant ministry of oversight in the Church of England and the Methodist Church and should be subject to normal ecclesiastical discipline

7.7.1 Fresh expressions, like every other part of the Church of England or the Methodist Church, are not independent ventures. Fresh expressions are accountable to the relevant ministry of oversight in the Church of England and the Methodist Church and should be subject to normal ecclesiastical discipline. In the Church of England this means that fresh expressions are accountable to the diocesan or area bishop and those who assist in the ministry of

183

oversight, archdeacons and rural and area deans. In the Methodist Church this means that fresh expressions are accountable to the Methodist Conference and those who assist in the ministry of oversight, which in most cases will be the circuit superintendent.

7.7.2   The requirement that fresh expressions conform to normal ecclesiastical discipline is a very sensitive matter in some quarters. A number of voices, frustrated with what they perceive to be unnecessarily restrictive 'controls', argue strongly that it is desirable in the case of fresh expressions to relax normal ecclesiastical discipline concerning the conduct of worship, preaching, and the celebration of the sacraments. Appeal is usually made to 'missiological reasons', though what these might be is not usually stated. There is a regrettable tendency to imagine that 'the needs of Christian mission' justify almost any development. However, there is little evidence to indicate that relaxing normal ecclesiastical discipline would in fact facilitate Christian mission. On the contrary, there is good reason to suppose that such a move would impair mission.

7.7.3   The ecclesiastical discipline of the Church of England and the Methodist Church exists to safeguard the integrity of the Church by ensuring that the Gospel is authentically preached and the sacraments duly administered by those authorized to do so. At stake here is nothing less than the apostolicity and catholicity of the Church. Ecclesiastical discipline is a sign of the connectivity of Christian communities with the universal Church in space and time. Fresh expressions, no less than any other Christian community, should be subject to normal ecclesiastical discipline (§5.7.11).

7.7.4   The effect of relaxing ecclesiastical discipline in the case of fresh expressions would be to compromise the integrity of the Church. Essentially, fresh expressions would become autonomous groups disconnected from others, except where voluntary alliances were formed. The ministry of word and sacrament present in them would be disconnected from that of the universal Church and its integrity thereby compromised. Such a state of affairs would be contrary to what the Church of England and the Methodist Church teach concerning the nature of the Church. The damage caused by failing to maintain normal ecclesiastical discipline in the case of fresh expressions would far outweigh any perceived gains from its relaxation.

7.7.5 In addition to safeguarding the integrity of the Church, normal ecclesiastical discipline also affords a measure of protection to all those involved in mission as representatives of the Church of England or the Methodist Church, as well as to those with whom they engage. Of course, any mission strategy involves a degree of risk: but it is for this very reason that ecclesiastical discipline should be upheld. For the usual risks involved in mission should not be compounded by setting aside measures intended to protect all parties. The Church of England and the Methodist Church would be negligent in their duty of safeguarding individuals if they allowed themselves to be persuaded that normal ecclesiastical discipline should not be maintained in fresh expressions. The potential problems of not doing so would represent an unacceptably high price to pay in return for doubtful short-term advantage.

7.7.6 While the normal ecclesiastical discipline of the Church of England and the Methodist Church should continue to apply in the case of fresh expressions, it should be applied in ways that take account of their circumstances and needs. This calls for a permissive interpretation of ecclesiastical discipline on the part of those charged with the ministry of oversight. It is impossible to legislate for a 'light touch' in applying ecclesiastical discipline. Only in a culture of mutual trust does such a 'light touch' become possible, where all parties are mindful of a shared responsibility to preserve and build up the Church.

7.7.7 A due process should be established whereby fresh expressions of church on the 'periphery' can be listened to by the 'centre'; a place for constructive dialogue where effective ecclesial practice emerging in response to the mission context of diverse localities is able to shape our shared dynamic tradition (§3.8.8, §6.7.2).

7.8 The development of fresh expressions requires authorized ministers with the necessary gifts and training

7.8.1   The development of fresh expressions requires pioneer ministers with the necessary gifts and training for Christian mission in the context of contemporary culture in Britain. This requirement presents the Church of England and the Methodist Church with a significant challenge in identifying suitable individuals, providing appropriate ministerial formation, and then deploying them to greatest effect.

7.8.2   Although the Church of England currently only recognizes ordained pioneer ministers, there is no reason in principle why the majority of pioneer ministers could not be lay people, though they would still require the necessary ministerial formation to be able to foster the ecclesial dynamics of intensivity and connectivity. If the normal discipline of the Church of England and the Methodist Church with regard to the celebration of the sacraments is still to apply, then a sufficient number of ordained ministers will also be required to provide a sacramental ministry for fresh expressions.

7.8.3   Few individuals are likely to possess all the necessary gifts for ministry in the complex mission context of fresh expressions. Those individuals who have the gifts to engage with contemporary culture and form new Christian communities amongst non-churched people may not possess the necessary skills in leading worship or teaching the faith. It may be desirable for the Church of England and the Methodist Church to establish ministry teams for fresh expressions. The pioneer minister or other designated leader

186

of a fresh expression within such a ministry team need not necessarily be the same person who exercises a sacramental ministry but ideally it will be someone who is undergoing or offering for ministerial training.

7.8.4   Pioneer ministers, as much as parish and circuit ministers, should encourage those new to the Christian life to develop spiritual disciplines that produce an appreciation of the Scriptures and the means of grace, especially the sacrament of the Lord's Supper. For this to happen, it is essential that pioneer ministers are themselves committed to those same spiritual disciplines, and that they have a sufficient knowledge of Scripture and Christian teaching concerning the sacraments.

7.8.5   Given that fresh expressions are still at a relatively early stage of development, the majority of pioneer ministers will continue to be drawn from traditional churches at least for the time being. It is important, however, that potential candidates for pioneer ministry are identified and cultivated within fresh expressions, just as overseas missions have long sought to produce indigenous ministers to replace external mission partners.

7.8.6   The Church of England and the Methodist Church are already developing training for pioneer ministry in fresh expressions and other contexts. The 'Mission-Shaped Ministry' course, part of the Fresh Expressions initiative, has proved to be a useful resource in this regard. Ministerial training is costly but necessary for safeguarding the integrity of the Church and its mission. The future development of fresh expressions will require a sufficient number of suitable pioneer ministers.

7.8.7   Given that the mixed economy is likely to grow in future, the Church of England and the Methodist Church will each need to establish an integrated strategy to recruit, train and deploy pioneer ministers and parish/circuit ministers. Such a strategy should allow for flexible patterns of ministry involving ordained and lay, stipendiary and non-stipendiary ministers (§6.4.7; §6.4.8). In all this the special needs of fresh expressions should be carefully considered (§6.7.2).

7.9 A mixed economy Church relies upon mutual trust, support and collaboration between traditional churches and fresh expressions

7.9.1 It cannot be stated too strongly that: A mixed economy Church should not mean parallel spheres of ecclesial life and mission having little in common. Nor should it merely denote a loose alliance of communities affiliated by adherence to a common objective. In a mixed economy Church each part belongs to every other part in such a way that there is one body. United with others in the one body of Christ, Christian communities should not think of themselves as competitors in mission but instead be willing to work together, sharing resources and insights for the good of the whole' (§6.4.1).

7.9.2 A mixed economy is not for its own sake but for the sake of engaging with people in their particular context. These contexts were identified in Chapter 6 as being based on neighbourhood, on social networks, and on 'locality' (a context that is neither exclusively territorial nor purely associational but relational and therefore inclusive of both). Localities overlap because people inhabit multiple spheres. Since there is one body of Christ, one Spirit, one faith, one Lord (Ephesians 4.4–6), there can only ever be one Christian mission. This means that mission in one context is not to be conceived or undertaken in isolation from mission in every other context.

7.9.3 A mixed economy requires a comprehensive mission strategy in which scarce resources of finance and people are used to greatest effect at the service of the Church's mission in the world. This requires spiritual discernment and active collaboration among all the various components, especially authorized ministers, who should be committed to listening to one another and praying together so that the mission of the Church may bear fruit (§6.4.2).

7.9.4 Mutual trust, responsibility and commitment are all needed within the structures that serve the mission and communion of the Church of England and the Methodist Church. In dioceses, deaneries and parishes, in districts and circuits, traditional churches and fresh expressions should support each other in a common mission as an effective witness to their unity and reconciliation in Jesus Christ.

7.9.5 A practical example of ministerial collaboration would be making provision for the regular celebration of the Lord's Supper in fresh expressions where an ordained minister is not readily available. It would be unfair to criticize fresh expressions for not encouraging sacramental worship if the deanery, parish or circuit does not make adequate provision for this to happen.

7.9.6 The ministry of oversight has a central role in facilitating active collaboration in a mixed economy. In the Church of England this ministry is exercised personally by bishops, archdeacons, rural deans and area deans. In the Methodist Church the ministry of oversight is exercised personally by district chairs and superintendent ministers under the corporate oversight of the Conference. It is important that all those who exercise a ministry of oversight should understand the purpose of fresh expressions and seek to promote a mixed economy within their specific area of responsibility.

7.9.7 Fresh Expressions Area Strategy Teams (FEASTS) provide a useful means of bringing together the various parties in a way that encourages collaboration rather than competition (§2.4.4). Other structures that already exist, and ones that might usefully be developed, should be encouraged at all levels to facilitate greater collaboration.

7.10 The wider implications of fresh expressions for the mission strategy of the Church of England and the Methodist Church require further investigation

7.10.1   The reasons why some fresh expressions are not sustained should be investigated so that scarce resources can be used to greatest effect in the Church's mission (§6.4.5).

7.10.2   The possible implications of fresh expressions for ecumenical relations and the unity of the Church should be investigated (§5.2.11). In particular, the Church of England and the Methodist Church may wish to consider whether increased ecumenical cooperation in the development of fresh expressions would give visible expression to their desire to work towards unity-in-mission in the spirit of the Anglican-Methodist Covenant.

7.10.3   The possible implications of fresh expressions for interfaith relations in Britain should be investigated in view of the commitment of the Church of England and the Methodist Church to maintaining good relations with non-Christian faith communities (§5.2.12) while still remaining committed to proclaiming the Gospel to all people.

7.10.4   The concept of inculturation of the Gospel requires consistent application in relation to mission in Britain (§5.8.12). The cumulative experience of Christian mission in Africa and Asia provide useful material for theological reflection in relation to mission and inculturation in Britain's multicultural and multi-religious society.

7.10.5   The implications of network society for Christian mission and the creation of fresh expressions in diverse 'localities' should be encouraged by the wider Church. (§5.4.15; §6.5.1) Their developing practice and experience should continue to be researched to shape our future mission.

7.11 Recommendations

7.11.1   The working party makes the following recommendations to the General Synod of the Church of England and the Methodist Conference concerning fresh expressions:

1. The Church of England and the Methodist Church should continue to support and resource the development of fresh expressions creating a mixed economy that epitomises the principles of connectivity and intensivity as set out in this report (§7.2).
2. The Church of England and the Methodist Church should, separately and together, continue to develop and implement mission strategies at all levels for a mixed economy in which fresh expressions and traditional churches work together in a common mission (§7.9).
3. The Church of England and the Methodist Church should work together to develop appropriate structures (including Fresh Expressions Area Strategy Teams) to support the implementation of their mission strategies by means of a mixed economy and in ways that encourage collaboration and mutual trust, commitment and responsibility (§7.9). This would be a practical outworking of the commitment to joint decision making contained in the Anglican-Methodist Covenant.
4. As part of a dynamic mission strategy, the Church of England and the Methodist Church should continue to monitor the changing nature of British society and learn from those called to mission and ministry on the periphery in diverse localities, assessing the implications for future mission (§3.8.2, §6.5.8).
5. Training for all ministers, especially pioneer ministers, should include among its aims the formation of individuals who will be able to relate the universal Church to local mission contexts. Such formation will necessarily require a deep knowledge and appreciation of Scripture, as well as an adequate understanding of the Anglican or Methodist tradition, as appropriate, and an awareness of its purpose in relation to Christian mission (§7.8).

6. The Church of England and the Methodist Church should develop a theological rationale and policy for identifying suitable candidates for ministry in fresh expressions, providing the necessary training, and deploying them according to a flexible pattern of ministry involving lay and ordained, stipendiary and non-stipendiary ministers. They should be adequately resourced and appropriately deployed to work effectively on the periphery in mission and ministry (§7.8).

7. The Church of England and the Methodist Church should consider how they might identify structures and personnel for dealing with those occasions when tensions arise concerning fresh expressions in a mixed economy Church (§2.1.10).

8. In the interest of accountability and safeguarding the integrity of the Church, the normal ecclesiastical discipline of the Church of England and the Methodist Church with regard to worship, preaching and the celebration of the sacraments should continue to apply in the case of fresh expressions; while a suitable place for dialogue and reflection should be created where the periphery and the centre meet to discern and authorize appropriate developments in ecclesial practice which reflect the Churches dynamic tradition as it advances in mission in the contemporary context (§6.7.2, §7.7.7).

9. Affirming that the Church has certain essential elements (§4.6.1; §7.3.5), the Church of England and the Methodist Church should adopt the following questions as a vocational 'health checklist' for traditional churches and fresh expressions:

   • Is this a community of people called by God who are committed to being disciples of Jesus Christ and living out their discipleship in the world?

   • Is this a community that regularly assembles for Christian worship and is then sent out into the world to engage in mission and service?

   • Is this a community in which the Gospel is proclaimed in ways that are appropriate to the lives of its members?

- Is this a community in which the Scriptures are regularly preached and taught?
- Is this a community in which baptism is conferred in appropriate circumstances as a rite of initiation into the Church?
- Is this a community that regularly celebrates the sacrament of the Lord's Supper?
- Is this a community where pastoral responsibility and presidency at the Lord's Supper is exercised by an appropriate authorized ministry?
- Is this a community that is united to others through: mutual commitment; spiritual communion; structures of governance, oversight and communion; and an authorized ministry in common?

10. The Church of England and the Methodist Church should continue to consider how they might work more closely together, and with other ecumenical partners, in developing fresh expressions.

11. The Church of England and the Methodist Church should continue to consider, both separately and together, the wider implications of fresh expressions for their mission and ministry (§7.10).

12. The Church of England and the Methodist Church should invest in the continuing catechetical, liturgical and spiritual formation of new Christians as committed disciples of Jesus Christ, enabling new disciples to be confident of their vocation to share fully in the mission of the Church (§6.2.5, §6.7.2, 7.7.7).

Appendix 1: Origins of the Working Party

The origins of the Joint Anglican-Methodist Working Party on the Ecclesiology of Emerging Expressions of Church lie in the 2007 Methodist Conference held in Blackpool. At that Conference a report was received which stated a number of questions relating to the current development of fresh expressions of church which required investigation:

The development of fresh ways of being church as part of a 'mixed economy' – valuing both the new and the established – raises questions which are as yet unanswered. How do we value and encourage both the new and the old while making room for the new? What is the relationship between a fresh expression and a Local Church, Circuit or District sponsoring it? How can we encourage a fresh expression to maturity? How can we station a minister who is called to develop a fresh expression? How can we test, recognize and enhance the ministries of the people God is calling to work in fresh expressions of church, particularly those pioneers not already ordained who have a proven track record of starting churches?

Further work in these areas is required. We therefore ask the Conference to direct the Methodist Council to ensure that the encouragement of new ways of being church in general and the work of the Fresh Expressions team continues to be properly resourced and supported. The Council should further ensure that the key issues being raised are addressed and appropriate guidance is brought to future Conferences.

The resolutions attached to this report led to the establishment of the Fresh Ways Working Party, which has the task of encouraging the development of fresh expressions throughout the Methodist Church, while also looking at their theological rationale and practical implications for the exercise of Methodist ministry.

In November 2007 the Methodist Faith and Order Committee discussed fresh expressions and whether or in what sense they can be regarded as manifestations of the Christian Church.

In light of the Anglican-Methodist Covenant and the commitment to joint working between the Methodist Church and the Church of England envisaged in the Anglican-Methodist Covenant, as well as the existing co-operation between Methodists and Anglicans in the *Fresh Expressions* initiative it was felt that further study of the subject of fresh expressions should be undertaken jointly by the Methodist Church and the Church of England. The Faith and Order Advisory Group subsequently agreed to accept this recommendation. Both churches then appointed their representatives to the Working Party, which held its initial meeting in February 2009.

At that first meeting it was established that that the specific task given to the Working Party is:

To undertake a critical study of the explicit and implicit ecclesiology of fresh expressions, and to produce recommendations or guidelines for ongoing work or change to existing structures that are workable within both traditions. These conclusions will seek to enhance our unity as one body in Christ, consistent with our traditions' understandings of the Church and interpretations of Scripture, while at the same time being alert to the new directions in which the Holy Spirit directs God's people. Such an ecclesiology should empower the Church's mission and resource the work of those involved in *Fresh Expressions*.

At the same meeting, the specific terms of reference given to the Working Party were tabled. The brief given to the working party was to:

- Describe and justify a theological method which takes into account current practice, innovation and entrepreneurship alongside traditional understandings of the Church and the Scriptures.
- Describe how certain terms, frequently used in this area with various shades of meaning, are to be used within this work: fresh expressions, emerging church, ecclesial community, fresh ways of being/doing church, inherited church, tradition, etc.
- Clarify the central questions that it intends to address (and, as appropriate, not to address).
- Identify and describe contemporary experience of, and issues in, ecclesiology, where necessary looking at how current social trends affect the existence of and development of mission communities.
- Reflect theologically on the findings of these enquiries. What results from the interplay between the different disciplinary insights? Where and when do theological insights challenge new practice? Where and when is inherited theology correctly challenged by current practice? How are clashes between the disciplines' reflections to be evaluated? How can the traditions of the Church appropriately counsel and shape emerging practices?
- Identify appropriate action and practice in the light of the analysis undertaken: holding together Scripture, reason and experience, to inform practice and pastoral care.
- Given that emerging churches, by definition, do not resemble inherited church structures, consider how the Church can most appropriately and effectively establish and support sacramental life in fresh expressions of the Church.

Appendix 2: Glossary of terms

Apostolicity
The *apostolicity* of the Church expresses its historical continuity with the mission and faith of the apostles.

Catholicity
The *catholicity* of the Church expresses the fullness, integrity and totality of its life in Christ through the Holy Spirit in all times and places.

Connectivity
Connectivity denotes those bonds of sacramental, spiritual and juridical communion that bind an individual Christian community to others within the fellowship of the universal Church.

Ecclesiology
Ecclesiology is that branch of Christian theology concerned with providing a theological account of the nature of the Church.

Emerging Church
In this report, *emerging church* refers to the phenomenon of post-denominational mission projects led by groups and individuals that are independent of the historic churches.

Fresh Expressions
Fresh Expressions is the ecumenical initiative supported by the Church of England and the Methodist Church as an agency for Christian mission to the non-churched.

fresh expression

A mission project sponsored by one of the denominations partici-pating in the Fresh Expressions initiative is referred to in this report as a fresh expression. According to the official definition, 'A fresh expression is a form of church for our changing culture, established primarily for the benefit of people who are not yet members of any church.'

Inculturation

Inculturation refers to the proclamation of the Gospel in a particular cultural context and using categories appropriate to that context.

Intensivity

Intensivity denotes those bonds of sacramental, spiritual and juridi-cal communion that bind individual Christians to one another in a particular Christian community.

Locality

Locality is defined in this report as a mission context that is neither exclusively territorial nor purely network-based but is relational and therefore includes both aspects.

Missio Dei

The *Missio Dei* is God's mission in the world in which the Church is called to participate.

Missiology

Missiology is that branch of Christian theology concerned with giv-ing a theological account of the mission of the Church.

Mixed economy

A *mixed economy* denotes a situation in which the life and mission of the Church is conducted in both traditional and new ways in order to meet the needs of different cultural contexts.

Non-churched

The term *non-churched* is used consistently throughout this report (except in direct quotations) to refer to those who have never belonged to the Church and are not members of other world religions. Some commentators use the term *unchurched*.

Pioneer Minister

A *pioneer minister* is a minister authorized and trained by the Church of England or the Methodist Church to work in developing fresh expressions.

VentureFX

VentureFX is an initiative of the Methodist Church to encourage the development of fresh expressions among young people.

Select Bibliography

Church of England Reports and Documents

Apostolicity and Succession (London: Church House Publishing, 1994).

Being Human (London: Church House Publishing, 2003).

Bishops in Communion (London: Church House Publishing, 2000).

Breaking New Ground: Church Planting in the Church of England (London: Church House Publishing, 1994).

Called to Witness and Service (London: Church House Publishing, 1999).

Common Worship Ordination Services, *Study Edition* (London: Church House Publishing, 2007).

'Celebrating Diversity in the Church of England: National parish congregation diversity monitoring' (General Synod, 2007).

The Eucharist: Sacrament of Unity (London: Church House Publishing, 2001).

The Homilies (Bishopstone: Brynmill Press/Preservation Press, 2006).

A Measure for Measures (London: Church House Publishing, 2004).

Mission-Shaped Church: church planting and fresh expressions of church in a changing context (London: Church House Publishing, 2004).

The Mystery of Salvation (London: Church House Publishing, 1995).

Sharing the Gospel of Salvation (GS Misc 956).

We believe in the Holy Spirit (London: Church House Publishing, 1991).

Methodist Church Reports and Documents

Called to Love and Praise: The Nature of the Christian Church in Methodist Experience and Practice (Methodist Conference, 1999).

A Catechism of the People Called Methodists (Methodist Conference, 1986).

Changing Church for a Changing World – Fresh ways of being Church in a Methodist context (Methodist Conference, 2007).

The Constitutional Practice and Discipline of the Methodist Church (Methodist Conference, 2010).

Encouraging fresh ways of being Church (Methodist Conference, 2004).

May I call you friend? Sharing Faith with People of Other Faith (Methodist Conference, 2006).

Methodist Worship Book (London: Methodist Conference, 1999).

The Nature of the Christian Church, in *Statements of the Methodist Church on Faith and Order 1933–1983* (Methodist Conference, 1984), pp. 5–42.

Statements of the Methodist Church on Faith and Order 1933–1983 (London: Methodist Publishing House, 1984).

Statements and Reports of the Methodist Church on Faith and Order 1984–2000, 2 vols (Peterborough: Methodist Publishing House, 2000).

Ecumenical Reports and Documents

An Anglican-Methodist Covenant (Peterborough and London: Methodist Publishing House/Church House Publishing, 2001).

Anglican-Moravian Conversations (London: Council for Christian Unity, 1996).

ARCIC, *Church as Communion* (London: Church House Publishing/Catholic Truth Society, 1991).

ARCIC, *The Gift of Authority* (London, Toronto and New York: Catholic Truth Society/Anglican Book Centre/Church House Publishing, 1998).

Called to be One Church (Geneva: World Council of Churches, 2006).

Churchgoing in the UK (Tear Fund, 2007).

The Meissen Agreement Texts (London: Council for Christian Unity, 1992).

The Porvoo Common Statement (London: Council for Christian Unity, 1993).

Secondary Sources

Alexander, Loveday, 'What patterns of church and mission are found in the Acts of the Apostles?', Steven Croft (ed.), *Mission-Shaped Questions: defining issues for today's church* (London: Church House Publishing, 2008), pp. 133–45.

Alexander, Loveday, 'Community and Canon: Reflections on the Ecclesiology of Acts', Anatoly A. Alexeev, Christos Karakolis, Ulrich Luz, & Karl-Wilhelm Niebuhr (eds), *Einheit der Kirche im Neuen Testament* (Tübingen: Mohr Siebeck, 2008), pp. 45–78.

Alexander, Loveday, 'Mapping Early Christianity', *Interpretation* 57/2 (2003), pp. 163–73.

Atkins, Martyn, *Resourcing Renewal: Shaping Churches for the Emerging Future* (London: Epworth Press, 2010).

St Augustine, *The City of God*, Philip Schaff (ed.), *Nicene and Post-Nicene Fathers*, First Series, Vol. 1 (Edinburgh: T&T Clark, 1994 [1886]), pp. 1–511.

Avis, Paul, *A Church Drawing Near* (London: T&T Clark, 2003).

Baker, Jonny *Curating Worship* (London: SPCK, 2010).

Bayes, Paul and Tim Sledge, *Mission-shaped Parish: traditional church in a changing context* (London: Church House Publishing, 2006).

Bockmuehl, Markus, *Jewish Law in Gentile Churches* (London: T&T Clark, 2000).

Browne, Harold, *An Exposition of the Thirty-nine Articles* (London: John W. Parker, 1854).

Calvin, John, *Institutes of the Christian Religion*, ed. John T. McNeill (Philadelphia: Westminster Press, 1960).

Chadwick, Owen, *From Bossuet to Newman*, 2nd edn (Cambridge: Cambridge University Press, 1987).

Coleman, Roger (ed.), *Resolutions of the twelve Lambeth Conferences, 1867–1988* (Toronto: Anglican Book Centre, 1992).

Cray, Graham, *Discerning leadership: Cooperating with the Go-Between God* (Cambridge: Grove, 2010).

Cray, Graham, Ian Mobsby and A. Kennedy, *New Monasticism as Fresh Expressions of Church* (Norwich: Canterbury Press, 2010).

Croft, Steven, *Starting a Fresh Expression* (London: Church House Publishing, 2006).

Croft, Steven (ed.), *The Future of the Parish System: Shaping the Church of England for the Twenty-first Century* (London: Church House Publishing, 2006).

Croft, Steven, 'What counts as a fresh expression of church and who decides?', Louise Nelstrop and Martyn Percy (eds), *Evaluating Fresh Expressions: Explorations in Emerging Church* (Norwich: Canterbury Press, 2008), pp. 3–14.

Croft, Steven, 'Formation for ministry in a mixed economy church', Louise Nelstrop and Martyn Percy (eds) *Evaluating Fresh Expressions: Explorations in Emerging Church* (Norwich: Canterbury Press, 2008), pp. 40–6.

Croft, Steven (ed.), *Mission-Shaped Questions* (London: Church House Publishing, 2008).

Croft, Steven, *Jesus' People: What the Church Should Do Next* (London: Church House Publishing, 2009).

Croft, Steven and Ian Mobsby (eds), *Fresh Expressions in the Sacramental Tradition* (Norwich: Canterbury Press, 2009).

Cyprian, 'Epistle LI', Alexander Roberts and James Donaldson (eds), *Anti-Nicene Fathers*, Vol. 5 (Edinburgh: T&T Clark, 1990 [1885]), pp. 327–335.

Davie, Grace, *Religion in Britain since 1945: Believing without Belonging* (Oxford: Wiley Blackwell, 1994).

Davison, Andrew and Alison Milbank, *For the Parish: A Critique of Fresh Expressions* (London: SCM, 2010).

Donovan, Vincent J., *Christianity Rediscovered: An Epistle from the Masai* (Maryknoll: Orbis, 1982).

Dunn, J. D. G., 'Is there evidence for fresh expressions of church in the New Testament?', Steven Croft (ed.), *Mission-Shaped Questions* (London: Church House Publishing, 2008) pp. 54–65.

Ford, David F., *Christian Wisdom: Desiring God and Learning in Love* (Cambridge: CUP, 2007).

Gamble, Robin, 'Doing traditional church really well', Steven Croft (ed.), *The Future of the Parish System: Shaping the Church of England for the Twenty-first Century* (London: Church House Publishing, 2006), pp. 93–109.

Gaze, Sally, *Mission-shaped and Rural: Growing Churches in the Countryside* (London: Church House Publishing, 2006).

Gibbs, Eddie and Ryan Bolger, *Emerging Churches* (London: SPCK, 2006).

Gonzalez, Justo L., *Acts: The Gospel of the Spirit* (Maryknoll: Orbis, 2001).

Gonzalez, Justo L., *The Changing Shape of Church History* (St Louis: Chalice Press, 2002).

Green, Laurie, *Let's Do Theology: A Pastoral Cycle Resource Book* (London and New York: Continuum, 1990).

Hooker, Richard, *Of the laws of ecclesiastical polity*, Book III ed. R. W. Church (Oxford: Clarendon Press, 1905).

Hope, Susan, *Mission-shaped Spirituality: the transforming power of mission* (London: Church House Publishing, 2006).

Hull, John M., *Mission-Shaped Church: A Theological Response* (London: SCM Press, 2006).

Hull, John M., 'Mission-shaped and kingdom focussed?', Steven Croft (ed.), *Mission-Shaped Questions: Defining issues for today's church* (London: Church House Publishing, 2008) pp. 114–132.

Hull, John M. 'Only one way to walk with God', Louise Nelstrop and Martyn Percy (eds), *Evaluating Fresh Expressions: Explorations in Emerging Church* (Norwich: Canterbury Press, 2008), pp. 105–120.

Irenaeus, 'Against Heresies', Alexander Roberts & James Donaldson (eds), *Anti-Nicene Fathers*, Vol. 1 (Edinburgh: T&T Clark, 1990 [1885]), pp. 313–567.

James, Graham, 'Mission and the Parish-Shaped Church', *Theology* CIX/847 (2006), pp. 3–11.

Kalt, William, and Robert Wilkins Henry, *The Emerging Church* (Washington DC: Regnery, 1968).

Lash, Nicholas, *Theology on the way to Emmaus* (London: SCM, 1986).

Leith, John H. (ed.), *Creeds of the Churches*, revised edn (Oxford: Blackwell, 1973).

Luther, Martin, 'On the Councils and the Church', Eric W. Gritsch (ed.) *Luther's Works*, Vol. 41 'Church and Ministry (3)', (Philadelphia: Fortress Press, 1966).

Meeks, Wayne A., *The First Urban Christians: The social world of the Apostle Paul*, 2nd edn, (New Haven and London: Yale University Press, 2003).

Metz, Johann Baptist, *The Emergent Church* (London: Crossroad, 1981).

Milbank, John, 'Stale Expressions: The Management-Shaped Church,' *Studies in Christian Ethics*, 21/1 (2008), pp. 117–28.

Mobsby, Ian J., *Emerging and Fresh Expressions of Church* (Westminster: Moot Community Publishing, 2007).

Morisy, Ann, *Beyond the Good Samaritan: Community Ministry and Mission* (London: Mowbray, 1997).

Nelstrop, Louise and Martyn Percy (eds), *Evaluating Fresh Expressions: Explorations in Emerging Church* (Norwich: Canterbury Press, 2008).

Newbigin, Lesslie, 'What is "a local church truly united"?', *Ecumenical Review* 29 (1977), pp. 115–28.

Newman, John Henry, *Essay on the Development of Christian Doctrine*, 6th edn (Notre Dame, Indiana: University of Notre Dame, 1989).

Outler, Albert C., 'The Wesleyan Quadrilateral – in John Wesley', Thomas C. Oden and Leicester R. Longden (eds), *The Wesleyan Theological Heritage: Essays of Albert C. Outler* (Grand Rapid: Zonderman, 1991).

Pearson, John, *Exposition of the Creed* (1659); revised by Temple Chevallier and Robert Sinker (Cambridge: Cambridge University Press, 1899).

Percy, Martyn, 'Old tricks for new dogs? A critique of fresh expressions', Louise Nelstrop and Martyn Percy (eds), *Evaluating Fresh Expressions: Explorations in Emerging Church* (Norwich: Canterbury Press, 2008), pp. 27–39.

Perham. Michael and Reeves, Mary Gray, *The Hospitality of God* (London: SPCK, 2011).

Platten, Stephen, 'Definitely *not* Church', *Theology* CX/853 (2007), pp. 3–9.

Platten, Stephen, 'The grammar of ministry and mission', *Theology* CXIII/875 (2010), pp. 348–56.

Powell, Gareth, 'A theological and sociological critique of the Mission Shaped Church report' (Unpublished Cambridge PhD Thesis, 2012).

Richter, Philip and Leslie J. Francis, *Gone But Not Forgotten: Church Leaving and Returning* (London: Darton, Longman & Todd, 1998).

Schreiter, Robert J., *Constructing Local Theologies* (Maryknoll: Orbis, 1985).

Shier Jones, Angela, *Pioneer Ministry and Fresh Expressions of Church*, (London: SPCK, 2009).

Smith, Alan, *God-shaped Mission: theological and practical perspectives from the rural church* (Norwich: Canterbury Press, 2008).

Taylor, John V., *The Go-Between God: The Holy Spirit and the Christian Mission* (London: SCM, 1972).

Telford, John, *The Life of John Wesley*, 4th edn (London: Epworth, 1924 [1906]).

Telford, John (ed.), *The Letters of the Rev. John Wesley A.M* 8 Vols (London: Epworth, 1931).

Tennens, Terry (ed.), *Journey into growth: The seven core values of a mission church* (London: Churches Together in Britain and Ireland, 2007).

Vanhoozer, Kevin J., *The Drama of Doctrine* (Louisville: Westminster John Knox Press, 2005).

Vanhoozer, Kevin J., 'A Drama-of-Redemption Model', Stanley N. Gundry and Gary T. Meadors (eds) *Four Views on Moving Beyond the Bible to Theology* (Grand Rapids: Zondervan, 2009), pp. 151–99.

Vickers, John A. (ed.), *A Dictionary of Methodism in Britain and Ireland* (Peterborough: Epworth, 1999).

Volf, Miroslav, *After Our Likeness: The Church as the Image of the Trinity* (Grand Rapids, Michigan: Eerdmans, 1998).

Walls, Andrew, *The Cross-Cultural Process in Christian History* (London: Continuum, 2002).

Walton, Roger, 'Have we got the Missio Dei right?' *Epworth Review*, 35/33 (2008), pp. 39–51.

Wells, Samuel, *Improvisation: The drama of Christian Ethics* (Grand Rapids: Brazos, 2004).

Wesley, John, Preface to 'Hymns and Sacred Poems' (1739), *The Works of the Rev. John Wesley* Vol. 14 (London: Methodist Conference, 1856).

Wesley, John, Sermon 74 'Of the Church', Albert C. Outler (ed.), *The Works of John Wesley* Vol. 3 (Nashville: Abingdon, 1986), pp. 45–57.

Wesley, John, 'The Nature, Design and General Rules of the United Societies in London, Bristol, Kingswood, and Newcastle upon Tyne (1743)', Rupert E. Davies (ed.), *The Works of John Wesley* Vol. 9 (Nashville: Abingdon Press, 1989), pp. 67–75 (p. 69).

Wesley, John, 'Journal', W. Reginald Ward and Richard P. Heitzenrater (eds), *The Works of John Wesley*, Vol. 20 (Nashville: Abingdon, 1991).

White, James F. (ed.), *John Wesley's Prayer Book: The Sunday Service of the Methodists in North America* (Akron, Ohio: OSL Publications, 1991).

Williams, Rowan, *Arius: Heresy and Tradition* (London: Darton Longman & Todd, 1997).

Williams, Rowan, 'Theological resources for re-imagining church', Steven Croft (ed.), *The Future of the Parish System: Shaping the Church of England for the 21st Century* (London: Church House Publishing, 2006), pp. 49–60.

Wright, Christopher J. H., *The Mission of God: Unlocking the bible's grand narrative* (Leicester: IVP, 2006).

Wright, N. T., *Scripture and the Authority of God* (London: SPCK, 2005).

Young, Frances, *The Art of Performance: Towards a Theology of Holy Scripture* (London: Darton, Longman & Todd, 1990).

Index